Hidden Manna

by
Rayola Kelley
and
Jeannette Haley

Published by
WinePress Publishing
MOUNTLAKE TERRACE, WA 98043

Cover artwork © Jeannette Haley

Edited by Chuck & Athena Dean

HIDDEN MANNA
© 1994 by Rayola Kelley and Jeannette Haley
Published by WinePress Publishing
P.O. Box 440
Mountlake Terrace, WA. 98043

Printed in Canada on recycled paper.

ISBN 1-883893-02X

Acknowledgement

There are countless individuals who helped make *Hidden Manna* possible. Let me begin by mentioning some committed supporters such as my parents, Lester and Ramona Kelley and our friends Lorrie Jones, Cheri Kuzmic, Noreen Walsh and Jo & John Thomson;without Archie Olson Sr., Lynne Humphreys and Chuck & Athena Dean, this book would not be.

Then there are those in the small community of Cascade, Idaho who helped pioneer this information when the Lord started to reveal it to me. Women with such names as Renae, Anita, Cheri, Dixie, Karen and Laurie not only subjected themselves to questioning, but tested it out on their families. Thank you for being willing to tread on new ground. Your willingness has touched many lives.

I must not forget those faithful pioneers in the state of Washington: Elaine Johnson, Joan and Mike Pray, Sondra Church, Chaplains Don and Elaine Adams, Pastor Bernie Sanders and Pastor Joe Fuiten. Thank you for coming through for us during our birth pangs.

I want to extend my appreciation to those who helped during the struggles and maturity of the ministry and writing of this book. Thanks to Jeff and Gloria Caulk, Jerry and Abby Foote, Kelly and Joan Davis, Mannix and Mary McDonnell, and Roxie Pace for coming along side as team members to hold up our arms. Pastor Dane and Sherrie Snyder and those encouragers of Cedar Park Church, and Bill and Vi Frederick, Judy and Gordon Emmert, Carol Stribling and Sharon Maldonado. Thank you for catching the vision and becoming an encouragement to Jeannette and myself. What a great bunch!

A special recognition must be extended to my co-laborer and helper, Jeannette. This information and book would not be, if it had not been for her unwavering support.

A special appreciation goes to my Precious Lord and Savior Jesus Christ. He has never forsaken me, even when I wanted to turn my back on Him during the rough times. He walked through every valley of uncertainty with me, and brought new life out of obscurity and failure. He brought light to those places where darkness lurked. He gave me comfort when sorrow was about to swallow me. He brought healing to the wounds, hope in times of despair, and understanding to chaos. He has proven to be faithful through every trial and, for whatever reason, He entrusted me with this nugget (the nature information).

Thank you Jesus, for saving my soul and for blessing me with the opportunity to watch this nugget set people free. You are indeed wonderful and all I can do is praise Your wonderful name and dedicate this book to You!

Rayola Kelley

Introduction

Manna has always been a mystery. The children of Israel knew how it looked and tasted, but didn't have a clue what it was made of. Even today, the very essence of what it was that God sent down to sustain His people remains a mystery.

You hold in your hands another form of God's manna. However, this one not only gives spiritual sustenance, but understanding as well.

When one thinks of the nature of people; images of personalities, childhood influences, temperaments and other acquired behaviorisms come to mind. But, as you will discover in this book, none of these have anything to do with the basic fabric God knit together when he made each one of us. Our nature is the primary, base ingredient that our Creator started with when He decided to form us into living souls. [Genesis 2:7]

In *Hidden Manna* the authors explain God's revelation to them about our "natures." They show us that there are only four natures throughout mankind. Christians will find this "manna" useful in becoming more godly people, as well as more effective ministers and witnesses.

This book will challenge you in many areas of your life. Have a wonderful journey as you discover your true fabric of the nature God created in you.

The Editors

Part One
Laying a Foundation

1

Human Nature Unveiled

What does it mean to be human? And how does the nature, that unchangeable essence of creation, affect us in our spiritual pilgrimage here on earth? It might serve us all well to consider these questions.

It appears as though many Christians are earnestly seeking the answer to these questions in order to understand themselves and others. They look to man's philosophies to make sense of the human journey of life--even in the church that Christ died for. In his great wisdom, the Apostle Paul warned Christians to avoid focusing on vain philosophies of man; and in fact, to look to man for anything is to lean on the arm of flesh.

In "Hidden Manna" we humbly submit to you these findings about the nature of four different types of human beings; how to recognize yourself in a respective nature; and, amongst other things, how to minister to other natures. We know that this information is not from the vain philosophies of man, and as we write this to you we lean solely upon the arms of Jesus.

We are excited to share our insights with you. Before we dive straight into the "nature" information, we would like to lay some necessary groundwork.

Developing the "Way"

We see that in relationships and spiritual matters many are victims of an invisible cycle they do not understand. Since understanding comes hard for some, they are perishing in the flood waters of hopelessness and despair, simply maintaining, rather than overcoming. Yet, 1 John 5:4 tells us, if we know Christ we are <u>overcomers</u>. A simple revelation, indeed, but from all observation the power of this truth escapes many in the Christian realm.

Families are falling apart, the church is full of strife on every level; and statistically speaking, is not far from the world in domestic problems and violence. Some churches, along with America, are being divided by the turmoil.

The question is how do you stop a bleeding artery or a train that is heading on a collision course? The answers are simple. Surgery is required for the bleeding artery, just like changing the course of a runaway train avoids impending disaster. However, what kind of surgery would it take to mend a broken soul? And what kind of change must occur to avoid the worst kind of destruction?

Christians know the answer. It is most simply and powerfully summarized in two words-- Jesus Christ. Jesus said He came to heal the broken hearted, and in John 14:6 He declares that He is the Way.

According to Vine's Expository Dictionary of Biblical Words, "way" not only means a pathway, but a course of conduct and a way of thinking. The person of Christ is the Christians' example of how they must conduct themselves in every situation. Yet, Christian conduct can only be manifested when the person has the mind of Christ. It is the "way"...the only way.

How do we develop this "way", or the attitude of Christ? The answer is simple, daily obedience to the Word of God within the boundaries of true worship mentioned in John 4:24. This means presenting ourselves as living sacrifices that lead us to this transformation of Spirit & truth.

The right spirit in the Christian life is the Holy Spirit. The Holy Spirit empowers us to live a Scriptural life, leading us into all truth. Without truth, a Christian will never develop the mind of Christ. The person of Christ can only meet us in truth. John 14:6 confirms this when Jesus declared, *"I am the Truth."*

According to John 8:32-36, the truth of Christ is what makes us free. This liberty is found in every facet of our life, whether it be the flesh, the emotional or the spiritual. 2 Corinthians 3:17 tells us where the Spirit is there is freedom (liberty). Therefore, the Holy Spirit and truth make up the cycle found in emotional and spiritual freedom.

Destructive cycles begin in man's flesh. The Apostle Paul declared that there was no good thing in the flesh. In Galatians 5:17 he tells us that the sinful nature (the flesh) is at war with the Spirit.

We must ask ourselves; does this mean that human nature is sinful? To understand this we must consider the fall of Adam. Because of Adam's actions in the garden, man is now encompassed within a fallen nature. Sin now works in and through human nature. What was first created in perfection has now been marred by disobedience. Traits that were exemplary of the Creator are now being perverted by the darkness of sin. Instead of knowing liberty man is now ensnared in the cycle of another spirit and the deception thereof. He is in fact a slave to this fallen, sinful nature.

Some Christians fail to see how sin abounds through them, even though they know the truth about Adam's fall. They see sin as a list of *dos* and *don'ts* while ignoring areas in their life which display carnality--not Christ.

One's spiritual condition is determined by whom they call master. If flesh is lord, sin reigns. If Christ is Lord, the fruit of the Spirit will be evident. Jesus confirms this when He stated, *"You shall know them by their fruits."* A Christ-like existence hinges totally on a person being led by the Spirit into all truth! To be Spirit led stipulates that Jesus Christ is the Master or Lord of a person's life.

The question is, how do I let Christ be Lord? Christ can only be Lord when all of our life is submitted to Him. This submission must take place on a daily basis. However, problems arise when the human nature subtly demands its way. Proverbs 14:12 states, *"There is a way that seems right to a man, but in the end it leads to death."* The subtlety of human nature is that its way seems right. In fact, the way of human nature can be very religious and logical. The nature can be motivated by the best intentions. It can feel, sound and look good; but, in the end the fruits of contention and strife will unmask its lordship in the person's life.

Isaiah 64:6 tells us, *"mans' best is as filthy rags."* The picture is clear. Human nature in its fallen condition is unacceptable to a Holy God. This truth became clear when Christ, who is God Incarnate, came to earth to become sin and die on a cross to redeem man. He came to once again restore mans relationship with his Creator. *(2 Corinthians 5:16-21)*

It is vital for Christians to determine who is reigning in their life. Although repetitious cycles imply something is lacking in their spiritual lives, some Christians have no idea how to get out of the cycle. They cannot distinguish their nature from true godliness.

The goal of this book is to perform major surgery on the present condition of each reader by changing the course of their nature. It is designed to help people understand their nature and to identify when it is reigning in their life. By understanding their nature, they can begin to take authority over it and bring it under the control of the Holy Spirit. By bringing their nature under the control of the Spirit, their lives will display Christ's life and attitudes to a skeptical world. Here is God's *"Hidden Manna."*

(Luke 4:18 &19; John 13:12-17; 16:13; I Peter 2:21-25; Philippians 2:5; Romans 12:1 & 2; 7:18 Matthew 7:15 & 16; Colossians 2:8)

2

Defining the Word "Nature"

When we hear the word "nature" we often think of the handiwork of God in the physical universe. But, it means more, and it is important that we begin to understand this word in relationship to God, man and sin.

Nature means <u>unchangeable</u> <u>characteristics</u> <u>which</u> <u>identify</u> <u>something</u>. According to Galatians 4:8 there is one God by nature. In other words, our God's identity does not hinge on His title of God, but rather His title describes His divine nature. The true God has characteristics that no other being or creature displays. Therefore, it is

7

reassuring to me to know that I must only please one God whose attributes will not change. He is the same today as He was yesterday and will be forever, and I can know this God intimately because He has given me His Written Word. Through this "word" I can clearly understand both His will and way because they will never contradict His nature.

Now let us consider human nature. Like the Creator, human beings have distinct characteristics which separates us from the rest of creation. Unlike God's nature which is singular, human nature has four different variations.

Each variation has different traits, different perceptions, different responses, and different forms of pride. In fact, these natures and their traits are so different that individuals are trapped in endless cycles of conflict and misunderstanding. By understanding the traits of these natures, one can begin to see how they inspire cycles of destruction.

These cycles begin when self, rather than God, is exalted as the answer to life's trials and tribulations. For instance, when we begin to rely on our intelligence, we are leaning on our own self or understanding. Yet, to depend on our knowledge is normal. The Apostle Paul made this statement in 1 Corinthians 1:26-27 about human knowledge: *"Brothers, think of what you were when you were called. Not many of you were wise by human standards; not many were of noble birth. But God chose the foolish things of the world to shame the wise..."*

The obvious question we must ask at this point is why is man's knowledge untrustworthy? The Apostle Paul gives us insight into the answer in 1 Corinthians 8:1-2, *"...We know that we all possess knowledge. Knowledge puffs up, but love builds up. The man who thinks he knows something does not yet know as he ought to know."*

Human knowledge is inspired by pride. Pride brings a perspective based on the world's standards and ideas. In contrast, the things of God are holy or set apart for His glory and purpose. For instance, acceptable knowledge is surrounded by godly virtues which keeps it in proper perspective. It must be put into practice which implies wisdom. Godly wisdom can be summarized by two words, Jesus Christ. Therefore, godly knowledge will ultimately lead us to the knowledge of Jesus Christ who is truth personified.

(1 John 2:16; 2 Corinthians 6:14-18; 2 Peter 1:4-8; 1; Corinthians 1:30)

Avoiding Misconceptions

What are some misconceptions about human nature? We ask this to challenge any frame of reference (mindset) which would serve as a block to receiving a fresh perspective on this priceless information.

Not Temperament Or Personality

The human nature information in this book is not associated with a person's temperment or personality. A person's nature inspires temperament or personality, but is not affected by them.

For example, an apple tree's growth or productivity will be influenced by the type of care it receives, and the environment in which it grows. Although it may never reach its full potential or produce apples, it still remains an apple tree by nature.

This is also true of man's nature. Much of a man's temperament or personality is influenced by upbringing and environmental stressors, but his nature remains constant and uninfluenced.

Today, people work hard to bring their temperament under control. However, before anyone can develop temperance in their attitudes and responses, they must bring their nature under the control of the Holy Spirit.

The Spirit's control over our nature comes before temperance. A *control* from within must be present before discipline can occur and manifest itself elsewhere in our lives. This is why meekness comes before temperance in the list of fruit of the spirit in Galatians 5:22-23.

It Must Not Be Associated With The Motivational Gifts

This teaching on human nature is not related to motivational or inherent gifts. However, we have found that the different traits of the four natures often determine the capabilities or emphasize the area of talents. (See Romans 12:3-8) For instance, one nature is very analytical. This trait can help process information in a logical way. This quality could be used in the area of teaching. Another nature is more emotional which can be used in the areas of mercy and service. Still another nature can be aggressive. As a result they make good administrators. The next can be visionaries, good at encouraging and planning for the future.

It is important to note that each nature is capable of being entrusted with any of the inherent gifts, but they have different approaches. There is nothing wrong with trying to discover our gifts. However, the real key to understanding and recognizing our inherent talents is accepting who we are in Christ. The reason acceptance is vital is because all too often we compare ourselves with others.

Because we do not display or execute our abilities as others do, we become stifled and unable to operate in our own gifts. By accepting ourselves, we can allow the Holy Spirit to bring forth our talents for the glory of God.

It Is Not Psychology

This information is not psychology. Psychology is the study of the mind and the behavior of man. Unlike psychology the human nature information is not an attempt to understand man's behavior. Instead this revelation explains the common denominators which inspire the cycles of human behavior.

Keep in mind, truth consistently works. We must consider the track record of psychology because we see it coming into the church. When examining this humanistic science, we need to ask two important questions. Can its established criteria be confirmed on a consistent basis? Can the origins be traced back to a worldly inspiration or from God's wisdom?

Psychology is, from all appearances, the world's answer to the overwhelming problems confronting our society. As Christians, we know there is only one answer to all problems, Jesus Christ. Therefore, how can we justify incorporating psychology into our mainstream beliefs without compromising the authority and power we have in Christ?

On the other hand, has the human nature information proven to be consistent? What are the fruits or results produced from this material? In seven years, the information has been verified by hundreds of people of all ages and groups. People who have put it into practice find solutions to problems and liberation from destructive cycles.

The problems in a person's life are created by sin. Until sin is confronted, the problems will

11

never be solved.

Since sin is the real offender, we need to understand how it works.

3

Identifying
the Culprit

Death means separation. Scripturally speaking, spiritual death means separation from God. This separation breaks fellowship between man and his Creator--and our sin is the culprit.

The traits that distinguish sin are deception and death. Hebrews 3:13 warns us about being hardened by the deceitfulness of sin. In Romans 6:23 we are told that, *"the wages of sin is death."* Therefore, we must know how to identify sin in our lives if we are to be victorious.

We all have different definitions of sin. Before proceeding, we must build a sturdy foundation to support the information being presented. In order to do that we will discuss some basic tenets of the Christian faith and will look at sin from God's perspective.

There are three ways in which God views sin;

"missing the mark."

Romans 3:23 declares that, *"all have sinned and come short of the glory of God."* Because of sin, man is missing God's salvation, love and mercy. It also means man is falling short of his designated potential. The second meaning of sin is:

"rebellion against God."

Rebellion is lack of respect for or opposition to authority. Man's rebellion opposes God's authority in his life. In 1 Samuel 15:23, we see God comparing the sin of rebellion to witchcraft.

To understand the implications of witchcraft, one must recognize its main goal which is *control.* By describing witchcraft in the simplest form we begin to see how the kingdom of darkness works.

Control means a person's thoughts, will and responses are ruled by another person's standards. These unobtainable standards rob a person of their dignity and bring confusion. Control demands total obedience but no amount of sacrifice will silence its appetite. The end result is oppression.

A good example of witchcraft is mind control. Those who openly practice sorcery use their mind to either control a person or bring about desired events. This control is accomplished through strong concentration or visualization. Some Christians unknowingly use the same form of control in order to get their way with God or to force their self-righteous way on others. This is indeed a dangerous state for a Christian.

When we realize rebellion takes control away from God, we understand we not only discard God's authority, but declare ourselves the final jurisdiction. This supremacy does not stop with self, but tries to take command over others. This brings us to the third definition of sin which is:

"doing it our way."

God's ways are higher. They comply with His nature of perfection and holiness. In comparison, Proverbs 21:8 tells us, *"man's ways are strange and perverted to God."*

Each individual sees their way of doing things as being right or normal. These personal standards are based on an individual's perception which is upheld and reinforced by his/her nature. Human nature gives the individual a false sense of control over their life and problems. Without God's intervention, life's best eludes them. Fear becomes a prominent companion as they struggle to gain some semblance of control in their life and relationship to others. As the grip of control become unbearable to those who come under its demands, battle of wills flare up between individuals or groups.

These battles are the products of sin in operation. Like a spider web, sin ensnares its helpless victims to await impending doom. Like cancer, it serves as a merciless terminal disease of the soul. With sin nothing is sacred and all will come under its dictates and demands. There is only one limitation to its path of destruction. We find this limitation in Romans 5:20, *"...But where sin increased, grace is increased all the more."*

God's grace is defined by an infinite love and inspired by an insatiable mercy that looks beyond man's pathetic state and seeks to establish

15

righteousness in his life. The Bible tells us, *"we are saved by God's grace and have hope because of His mercy."*

It is God's grace and mercy which breaks the cycle of sin and brings salvation to the lost and hurting. But, how do we tap into His unlimited resources? The answer rests with honesty and separation. (*Ephesians 2:4-10*)

The Foundation of Sin

We are faced with a constant battle living in the reality of the world.

There are three world systems mentioned in the Bible. The first is that of creation. The second is directed toward humanity, *"for God so loved the world."* The third system is the one we will consider--the world as it relates to Satan's systems.

These systems include oppressive and controlling governing bodies and organizations. The Scripture is clear, if we are friends with these systems, we are enemies of God. I John 2:15 & 17 commands us, *"not to love the world for it will pass away, but those who do the will of God shall live forever."*

It is easy to tell people to be 'in the world but not a part of it.' Being part of the world means Satan and his deceptions influence our lifestyles as well as our thoughts. We are commanded to have the mind of Christ which Philippians 4:8 vividly describes as humility, single mindedness, obedience and rejection of evil at every level.

Some Christians give the appearance of separation from the world, but are very much a part of the world because of their carnal mind. If the carnality of the mind is not transformed and brought under the control of the Spirit, spiritual failure is inevitable.

During my time in the United States Navy, I was stationed at Pearl Harbor, Hawaii. I lived on a well known street called Hotel Street. This street was a hodgepodge of people from various backgrounds. Some lived there, others came on business, still others were there for brief pleasures. As I observed the flow of people along Hotel Street I was able to distinguish four types of people: victims, associates, pleasure seekers and tourists. I see similarities between how Christians respond to the world and these four groups.

The Victims

I remember looking up into a window of an old dilapidated building. In one of the windows was a beautiful Hawaiian girl. She was no more then six years old. Her hopeless eyes held my attention. I felt those eyes had beheld more in her short time then I had in all my 20 years. What had she seen?

I was quite aware of what she witnessed. Her world was comprised of derelicts, alcoholics, drug addicts and prostitutes. They had all become helpless victims of a dead end street which led to destruction.

Backslidden Christians are the "victims" in the Christian realm. Having witnessed God's greatness and turned aside, they are haunted by the fear that they may have gone too far for God to forgive them. They live in a world of despair and grief, believing a lie and above all else--fearing God's rejection.

Hope and forgiveness is a prayer away, but unbelief and fear paralyzes them. Promises are close, but their spiritual eyes have been blinded by the god of this world. Therefore, they cannot perceive or appropriate God's assurance that He even loves backsliders.

The Associates

The second group of people did not want to be identified with the dregs of Hotel Street. They were the pimps and owners of establishments such as taverns, burlesque and triple X-rated theaters who used people's circumstances and appetites for their own gain.

Associates in the Christian community want to make it to heaven, but they want the benefits of the world. The world's ways can be compared to swine. Pigs prefer to wallow in mud and eat garbage. They are complacent until someone invades their territory.

Those who consider Christianity only for the purpose of avoiding hell may be compared to swine. They want the benefits of both Christianity and the world without paying the price of separation from the world. The truth is--a pig smells like a pig. Those who try to have one foot in the heavenly realm and one in the world will inevitably smell and act like the world. They might fool some of the people some of the time, but they cannot fool them all of the time. As these individuals are challenged, they resent and reject the real nuggets of God's Word, thereby coming under God's judgment.

The Pleasure Seekers

When aircraft carriers arrived in port, sailors swarmed to Hotel Street for an evening of fun and pleasure. But the fun was temporary and the men left their money, integrity and dignity behind. Like the sailors, there are Christians who want to enjoy the world's pleasures for a time before they get serious about living a separated life. They feel they are missing something, a lie which is from the god of this world.

The problem with sin is that it always leaves some residue behind to haunt you. Somehow you will know you had an audience to witness your activities and your sins will find you out.

The Tourist

Sightseeing tourists are the fourth group traveling on Hotel Street with no intention of stopping, because they have more important destinations. They simply pass through the tragedy of Hotel Street without personally experiencing it.

Christian sojourners, like the tourists, are passing through this world. Their destination is the city built by the hands of God. Their priority is to be faithful in service to their King and Lord. Their attitude is inspired by the knowledge that they are a citizen of heaven, and they have the official title of Ambassadors of Christ. They know the world holds nothing and they have left all to experience an eternity with their precious Lord.

Consider the four groups. Which one best describes your response to the world? If you respond as a victim, an associate or a pleasure seeker, then you have opened a door to Satan who will come in to oppress and destroy.

(Jeremiah 3:14; Matthew 7:6; Luke 12:35-48; John 3:16; 14:30; 15:18-22; 16:11; Romans 8:7; 12: 1 & 2; 1 Corinthians 3:11; 2 Corinthians 5:20; 10:3-6; Ephesians 6:5 8; Philippians 3:7-11, 20; 1 Timothy 6:3-10; Hebrews 11:8 & 9; James 4:4; 1 Peter 2:11)

The Root of Sin

The love of God is the root of Christianity. Roots determine the quality of the fruit. In the case of our spiritual life, our heart condition and our mind represent the root system.

Much work must take place in our heart and mind before we can manifest the life of Christ. This transforming work includes death to, or separation from, self rule and control. It involves regeneration and a new life that will be an expression of Jesus Christ.

Scripturally, we see the description of this new life summarized in Ephesians 4 & 5; Philippians 3 and Colossians 3. This new existence comes from loving God with all our heart, soul, mind and might. It is inspired by the sincere desire to please Him and Him alone, and is submissive in response. It is faithful to Christ's Lordship--at all times.

Now we must consider the root of sin. What motivates a person to act independently of God's authority? James 3:16 gives us a clue with this declaration, *"For where you have envy and selfish ambition, there you find disorder and every evil practice."*

To understand the implications of this text, we must consider Satan's temptations which are designed to entice man away from his Creator. The Apostle John verified this in his explanation of the world's makeup in 1 John 2:16, *"For everything in the world--the cravings of sinful man (the flesh), the lust of the eyes and the boasting of what he has and does--comes not from the Father but from the world."*

The temptation of Jesus in Matthew 4 and Luke 4 illustrates how Satan's appeal to flesh, pride and vision may seem rational, correct and wise.

Flesh

For instance, the bread was a temptation to Jesus' flesh. Galatians 5:19-21 draws a clear picture of the cravings of the flesh. They are sexual immorality, impurity and debauchery, idolatry, witchcraft, hatred, discord, jealousy, fits of rage, selfish ambition, dissensions, factions, envy, drunkenness, orgies, etc.

Pride

The second temptation of Jesus involved his pride. He was the Son of God; why not prove it? It would be natural for any normal man to accept Satan's dare to prove his identity and importance. Praise be to God that Jesus was no "normal" man!

Vision (Authority)

The third temptation entailed Jesus taking His rightful position of authority over all the kingdoms of the world. Since He was shown the magnitude of these kingdoms, his vision was being tempted.

Hebrews 4:15 confirms that Jesus was tempted in all three areas, and yet did not sin. Now consider for a moment that Jesus' submission to any of these suggestions would seem normal by human standards. However, in each case Jesus refused to submit to the temptation by quoting the Word of God.

Now we must ask ourselves, what was Satan really asking Jesus to do? In the first temptation, Satan was asking Jesus to look to the world for His strength. We know God is our provider and it is only by waiting upon God and relying on His Word will we know a sustaining and eternal strength. Jesus substantiated this truth in His response to Satan when He said of Himself in the Gospel of

John, *"I am the bread of life...I am the giver of Living Water."*

If Jesus had sucumbed, He would have been making Satan the provider and sustainer of His physical life. This would have brought His soul under subjection to the god of this world. Remember, rebellion is acknowledging something or someone other than God as your only authority. In this case, the flesh would have become Jesus' ruler.

In the second temptation Satan invited Jesus to, 'Prove you are God.' Why should God prove His identity? His very creation verifies His existence and nature. Jesus referred to this enticement as putting God to a foolish test; and He refused.

A believer, without intention, can put God to a similar test. This test can occur when man asks God to prove Himself by complying with the person's whims or ideas. To avoid falling for this temptation our motives must be right. In order to be assured of correct motives, we must love God more than ourselves. The Apostle Paul showed what our goal must be at all times when he stated, *"we must only boast or glory in the Lord."* Where does an individual's faith rest in such a test, with himself (pride) or with God?

In the final temptation we see Satan offering Jesus all the earthly kingdoms. Satan was enticing Jesus' eyes. Eyes represent vision and the soul of man. Satan was asking Jesus to take His vision off the heavenly realm and put it on the world. Can you begin to grasp the real temptation of Jesus? It was not time for Christ to take His rightful position as King. Christ had to go to the cross. His Father had set the time of preparation for his suffering and death. Christ could have ignored his Father's timing, but he chose to submit. There are believers who know God's plan for their lives, but refuse to wait for God's perfect timing. They do not want to go through the preparation. They resent suffering and their earthly vision refuses to accept the concept of death to self. They push ahead of God's plan. In essence, they are saying, 'I <u>will</u> bring forth God's perfect will according to my timing.' However, God's time is based on eternal purpose, not earthly convenience.

Idolatry

Once again we must ask ourselves, who is being exalted in each temptation? The answer is simple: man. The next question is who would Christ subject Himself to if He had submitted? Satan, of course.

Submission to anybody but God is the sin of idolatry. Idolatry breaks the first two commandments. It says "God's rules do not apply here." Therefore, God ceases to be ruler and takes a back seat to someone or something else in my life. Although we tend to put idolatry in the category of lesser sins, to God it is the root cause for all sins. If we truly love God in the fashion He deserves, we can <u>wait</u> for His perfect <u>timing</u> because we <u>know</u> Him. He is our strength, the author and finisher of our faith and the ruler of the universe. He alone deserves our adoration and commitment. He is our wisdom, sanctification, righteousness and redemption.

What do the fruits of your life say about your root system? Are you being ruled by a complete love for God or by the sinister root system of idolatry which deceives and destroys?

(Psalm 119:28; Isaiah 40:31; Daniel 11:32; Matthew 6:22-24; John 4:13; 6:32-35; 7:37-39; Romans 1:20; 1 Corinthians 1:30)

Genuine Repentance

One cannot talk about sin without making reference to repentance. II Corinthians 7:10 states that there are two types of repentance. One kind of repentance is known as **worldly sorrow**.

Worldly sorrow is man's way of dealing with sin. A good example of worldly sorrow is Judas Iscariot. In Matthew 27:3 & 5 we see where Judas repented of betraying Christ. He admitted to the religious leaders he had falsely accused an innocent man. He gave back the thirty pieces of silver. When the pious leaders responded callously, Judas took the matter of his sin into his own hands. He felt so much remorse that he went out and hung himself.

This act may have seemed noble but there was no acknowledgment of his need for God's forgiveness. The teachers of the law declared only God can forgive sins in Mark 2:7. Because God is the sole judge of our souls, this would make them correct. I John 1:9 confirms this with the promise that *God is just and able to cleanse those who confess their sins from all unrighteousness.*

Confession means you are in agreement with God that sin breaks fellowship with Him. However, true repentance goes beyond worldly sorrow and verbal confession. It involves a complete change in three areas of our life.

An About Face

II Peter 3:9 gives us an insight into real repentance by stating it is God's will that all come to repentance. Acceptable repentance leads to salvation while worldly sorrow ends in destruction. True repentance implies one is becoming accountable for their deeds. Without such accountability, there will be no awareness of a need to change.

This change involves an alteration of the heart, mind and response. King David made reference to a heart and mind change in Psalm 51:10 when he asked God to *create within him a new heart and an upright spirit.* We first must acknowledge that sin is based on God's definition of it in His Word. This acknowledgment starts with the mind being changed about personal sinful actions. This change is not an emotional outburst like the one Esau had when he sold his birthright for food. Once the mind comes into subjection and agreement with God, the heart must concur by changing both its desire and attitude.

The heart must desire to please God and develop a hatred for deeds which bring separation from Him. This hatred is given only when the person submits to the Holy Spirit. An acceptable heart response indicates that one has the fear of the Lord, which is the beginning of wisdom.

Once the heart is changed, the right response will follow. Many people have changed their direction without experiencing a change of heart or mind. This is not genuine repentance.

True repentance involves reconciliation with God. Reconciliation is the New Testament definition and work of atonement. This new work entails restoration, which not only includes coming to the cross for forgiveness, but receiving God's forgiveness. Remember, Jesus paid the price for our sins on the cross. Therefore the work of atonement is more than the covering of our sin, it is the complete work of redemption which results in us once again being reunited in a relationship with our Creator. Reconciliation can only occur when there is a broken heart and a contrite spirit.

Scripture is adamant that God can only respond after man correctly responds to Him. For instance, God can only begin to draw near to us when we draw near to Him. He can only forgive us after we confess our sins. He will only reveal Himself to us after we have searched for Him in spirit and in truth. Therefore, Christianity is a walk of faith which is obedience with the expectation of seeing God meet us in every need and situation because He does not lie.

Real repentance always means accountability for our actions, attitudes, desires and priorities. It goes beyond emotions to the very depths of man's heart. As Jeremiah 17:9 & 10 declares *no one knows the heart or mind of man, but God.*

(Psalm 34:18; 51:17; 111:10; 2 Corinthians 5:18-21; Philippians 2:12; Hebrews 12:14-17)

5

Repentance vs. Human Nature

Since human nature is encumbered with a fallen nature, it rejects true repentance. This rejection is enhanced by deception which is inspired by the sin factor.

When human nature encounters sins, failures or problems, it quickly resorts to its own understanding. It actually exalts itself to the place of lordship.

This subtle promotion is reinforced by a deceptive attitude which convinces the person that they can control or change the situation. These attitudes are expressed three ways.

Attitude #1
I will deal with it, leave me alone.

An individual with this reaction deals with each challenge as a card dealer would a deck of cards. Each situation is considered separately. To escape confusion they avoid seeking the advice of others because they have their own way of gaining understanding. In the end, they lose perspective and become surrounded in a shroud of confusion and doublemindedness within their narrow world.

Attitude #2
I will handle it, I'll prove it to you.

This person has two responsibilities. First, they must handle the problem. Secondly, they must prove to everybody else that they can handle it no matter what may confront them.

A good example of how this individual appears to handle every situation can be compared to the Titan, Atlas, holding up the world. Although this individual tries hard to handle everything, eventually they become overburdened and frustrated.

Attitude #3
I will take care of it, I'll show you

This person has two responsibilities as well. They must show you that they can take care of any problem by solving it. Of course, their way of solving a problem often implies others must comply with their solutions. This demand for compliance causes frustration, resentment and conflict.

Ultimately people trapped by these attitudes discover they have no real power to change the situation. You might assume that Christians would recognize their spiritual poverty. Some do and repent, but those who do not go on to the next stage: rebellion.

Rebellion on the Throne

Rebellion may be expressed as withdrawal, justification or self-righteousness. When people withdraw they may scold themselves or rationalize that they are actually innocent victims of the situation.

A good example of withdrawal may be observed in the life of the prophet Elijah. Elijah had just scored a victory over the prophets of Baal. But in his heightened state, he heard the death threats Jezebel made against him. Instead of remembering how God honored him on Mount Carmel, he focused on Jezebel's promise to destroy him. Because he felt like a victim, he retreated to the desert.

Elijah's real enemy was not Jezebel but fear. Elijah's fear was in control, not God. What did he fear the most? If Jezebel was able to carry out her threats, whose reputation was on the line - God's or Elijah's?

Instead of drawing near to God, Elijah withdrew into his own pathetic world. His fear let him off the hook and gave him the right to display anything but trust in his great God. After all, God had let him down. He was alone in his predicament. He did not recognize that fear is a lie. But praise God, God was gracious enough to pursue Elijah and eventually put things in perspective for him.

Another means of protecting self is justification. Instead of being accountable for personal actions, the individual blames others.

A good example of this practice can be observed in the life of King Saul. Saul had clear instructions concerning the Amalekites in 1 Samuel 15. By allowing the king to live and keep the best of the flocks, Saul went against God's instructions. When the prophet, Samuel confronted the King Saul implied the men kept the animals with the intention of offering them to God.

In response to Saul's feeble excuse, Samuel said, *"Does the Lord delight in burnt offerings and sacrifices as much as in obeying the voice of the LORD? To obey is better than sacrifice, and to heed better than the fat of rams."*

Romans 5:1 & 9 tells us, *"we are justified by faith, through the precious blood of Jesus."* There is no other means of justification. Those who use man's avenue of justification will still answer to God for their own actions and decisions on judgment day.

The third reaction to avoiding personal accountability is to factually and logically **make it right in their own eyes.** We see this type of response coming from the people of Israel during the time judges ruled over them.

The problem with this type of response is that an individual can begin to call evil - good, and good - evil. It becomes a form of delusion which will bring judgment.

Proverbs 16:2 declares, *"a man's ways seem right to him, but God weighs the spirit."* Isaiah 64:6 states, *"man's best is considered as dirty rags before God"* and Romans 3:10 tells us, *"there is none righteous."*

There is only one source that makes us right before God, the blood of Jesus. 1 Corinthians 1:30 tells us, *"Jesus is our righteousness;"* therefore, we can only stand acceptable when Christ is in us. It is His presence in us that is our only hope of glory.

It is obvious that man's attempts to cover his own frailties are insufficient to atone for sin. Jesus became the whipping boy; the sacrifice and sin for each of us so that we could be cleansed from all unrighteousness and escape the fires of hell. With this in mind, how do you think God views it when we whip ourselves, sacrifice the other guy, or make self right in our own eyes? Is it any wonder that hell awaits those who insist on making themselves right without looking to God's provision of Jesus Christ?

(Judges 17:6; 21:25; 1 Kings 18:16-19:218; Isaiah 5:14-16, 20; Matthew 5:3; Colossians 1:27; 1 John 1:7)

6

The Motivation Behind Human Nature

Why doesn't man simply come to true repentance? It would appear to be the easiest route to pursue, but man avoids it. Why? Because there are two opposing forces influencing man, God or love of self (pride).

Pride motivates those whose lord is not Jesus Christ. It is the opposite of God's love defined in 1 Corinthians 13. Strife and contention are its predominate by-products.

Pride represents the condition of a man's unregenerated heart.

Since most people have their own definition of pride, we need a common understanding of this sin. I have two definitions. Perhaps they will help you too. The first one:

"exultation of self."

Exultation means you have become superior. In order to be superior, someone must become inferior. To determine who belongs in either category implies you have placed yourself in the position of being a judge over others. This is the opposite of Jesus' instruction found in Matthew 7:1-6.

God is the only real judge of man and Scripture declares He does not show any favoritism. Therefore, how can mere man exalt himself above others of his species? James identifies this type of judgment as unmerciful.

In order to establish superiority one must develop a set of standards for judging others. These standards are based on influences such as religion, culture and upbringing, and create an idea of self, which comprises the second definition of pride:

"an image of self."

This image or idea of self is made up of high opinions. These high opinions serve as superior judgments. These judgments become burdens to others because man cannot empower anyone else to live up to his/her ideas. In essence, victims of these standards are required to bow down to an image (our pride). This is why 1 Samuel 15:23 refers to *arrogance as being the same as idolatry* in the NIV.

God calls us to honor Him. He has given us the Holy Spirit who empowers us to live the

Christian life. Instead of bowing down to some unrealistic image, we are called to bow down to a real live entity. We know this entity to be God of the Bible, the Creator of the universe who never changes.

Right now consider what motivates you: God's love or pride. If pride is your motivation, you need to know God is resisting you.

Friends of Pride

Pride gives an impression of infallibility. But in the midst of the reign of pride, you can catch glimpses of things which are inconsistent with its nature. These inconsistencies are created by the influential friends of pride.

The first associate of pride is **fear**. Arrogance cannot afford to be wrong; it cannot fail; it cannot bear to display weakness or to be rejected. Therefore, fear of failure and rejection keeps an individual from becoming accountable for any weakness. Such weakness means we are vulnerable. Vulnerability implies inferiority, a state we dare not acknowledge.

II Timothy 1:7 tells us fear hinders three major areas in our spiritual life. These are love, power and a sound mind.

I John 4:18 states *"perfect love drives out all fear."* The reason that fear stifles love is because we fear God's reaction to us. We fear punishment; therefore, we are not open to forgiveness. This paralyzes us from receiving God's grace and mercy.

Fear also inspires another friend of pride which is **unbelief**. The power that 2 Timothy 1:7 refers to is the supernatural power of God. To have this miracle-working power one must have faith.

Faith lets God be God. Hebrews 11:6 confirms this definition. It is trusting God to be *"who He is."* This trust entails having a revelation or intimate knowledge of God's identity. This identity allows us to know His ways and His will for our life. This knowledge of our great God gives us faith that is capable of moving mountains.

On the other hand, pride will never allow God to be God. Pride serves as god and the individual must lean on their own understanding to contend with situations. Since God is never allowed to be God, the person will never come to any real knowledge of Him. This lack of intimacy will create a vacuum of unbelief in the powerful Creator.

A good example of this vacuum is found in the children of Israel. Even though they had witnessed great miracles, they did not believe God because they did not know Him in a personal way. Therefore, they were unable to trust his provision to enter the promised land.

Fear also produces an unsound mind. This brings up the third associate of pride which is confusion.

I Corinthians 14:33 tells us, "*God is not a God of confusion, but of order*." Confusion inevitably occurs when reality contradicts our image of self. This contradiction creates unrest in our soul and doublemindedness in our thinking.

James 1:8 gives us an insight about doublemindedness by declaring that it, "*makes a man unstable in all his ways*." In this state of mind people appear to walk a fine line between sanity and insanity. Not only are these individuals perplexed about their identity but they send mixed messages to those around them.

This brings us to the identification of pride's fourth friend, delusion. Since pride is a sin and sin carries with it deception, delusion is the natural by-product. Jeremiah 49:16 talks about the proud heart which is deceived. We cannot bear to be wrong; so, we con ourselves into believing we are the person we desire to be.

Romans 12:3 instructs us, *"to not think of ourself more highly than we ought, but to examine ourself in a sober manner."* Deception represents the road of least resistance. Truth symbolizes the hard and narrow path. Most prefer the lie and many avoid the truth. It is easy to give in to delusion, but the end result is destruction.

Therefore, we cannot afford to give in to pride and its friends. They are untrustworthy and will only bring temporary relief. They set us up for a fall and ultimately, will expose in us the very things we strive to avoid.

The truth is, without Christ we are failures. It is His grace which keeps us from being vulnerable to sin. It is His love which subdues rejection in our lives. It is His Spirit which empowers us to be successes in the kingdom of God.

The question is, why does man refuse to face this truth? What is he really hiding? Is he so deceived that truth remains far from him? The answers rest in man's need to belong and his desire to control his environment.

(Proverbs 13:10; 28:25-KJV; Matthew 17:20; Luke 9-14;Acts 10:34; Hebrews 3-5; James 1:17; 2:2,13; 4:6; 1 Peter 5:5 & 6 refer to Matthew 11:28-30)

In Pursuit of Fulfillment

People do not start out on a pride trip. They have one of three basic desires, which are:

to experience love;
to experience peace;
to experience joy or happiness.

These desires are based on what is happening in their relationships and environment. For instance, if someone desires love there may be a great deal of hatred in their environment. If a person wants peace, they are telling you their life is full of turmoil. If an individual desires joy or

41

happiness, they are contending with hopelessness and despair.

All human beings have one of three basic needs. They are:

> to be loved;
> to be accepted;
> to be recognized.

These needs are always based on the person's nature and give people a sense of belonging. By belonging, an individual has both purpose and direction.

In today's world it is not unusual to hear people question their reason for living or purpose in life. As a result, drugs, alcohol and gang association may become a desperate substitute for some, while others look to material possessions, the workplace, or causes to lend substance to their existence. Is there any way to solve the problem? The answer is yes. We must somehow give individuals what they need.

There is a stumbling block to successfully meeting another person's needs. That block is differences in the way people recognize their needs being met. For instance, we all have our own idea of loving someone. This standard is often based on childhood experiences and our definition of emotional commitment. Although we try to communicate our love to someone we may be unsuccessful because our way of giving love and their way of receiving it are different. Instead of meeting a need, we unintentionally create a point of contention in our relationship with them. We must learn to meet people's needs based on their perception of the need not our own.

Unfortunately, there are always those who refuse to submit to such a concept. Instead of seeing the benefits of filling a valuable need in the life of their spouse, they see this as giving in to their partner's whims. This unwillingness to concede comes from pride.

Pride refuses to be subject to anyone. It demands its own way. It wants to rule and be recognized. Therefore, basic needs are not being met. This becomes a point of contention between individuals.

The individual with the need becomes frustrated. They see the other person's unwillingness as a lack of commitment. After all, they entered this relationship looking for a way to have their needs met. Since the individual has a genuine need, they must figure out a way to have it fulfilled. It is at this point that control and manipulation enter the picture.

There are three forms of control and manipulation:

words;
attitudes;
actions.

When people use these forms of control in their relationships, struggles begin because others in the relationship resent being manipulated. What started out as a simple pursuit for fulfillment ends up in a battle where wills collide and destructive cycles gain momentum. This battle is nothing more than self, struggling to subdue and control another. The real issue of meeting needs is lost in the struggle.

Regardless of who overcomes in this war, there are no winners...just casualties. Relationships and lives become disrupted and sacrificed as the god of self relentlessly demands its own way.

The answer to this problem is simple, but everything in human nature rejects the solution because it is totally contrary to the survival of self.

Application of the Cross

We read in the preamble of the United States our godly forefathers' recognition of man's God-given right to have liberty in their endeavors and to enjoy a fulfilling life without restraint or oppression. I believe they felt God created man with a basic need to belong and a desire to experience bliss in life. The reason for this is obvious. God desires to draw people back into a relationship with Him but man must have the right, at all times, to choose to be reconciled back to his Creator.

Scripture tells us God is <u>love</u>. Because of the work of Christ on the cross, we are <u>accepted</u> in the beloved. We have <u>recognition</u> due to our position as God's special people who serve as His temples, priests and ambassadors. Christ is our <u>peace</u> and He brings unspeakable <u>joy</u> to our lives. And <u>happiness</u>, we are told in Matthew 5, only comes when attitudes are right. Right attitudes are inspired when we have a right relationship with God.

According to 1 Corinthians 6:20, *we have been bought with a price.* This means we <u>belong</u> to God. Since we belong, we can now establish the purpose behind our existence by understanding why God created man in the first place.

God brought forth Adam from the dust to be in <u>fellowship</u> with Him and to <u>glorify</u> Him. Fellowship gives us purpose, brings honor to our Creator and provides us with direction.

Truly, all of our needs and desires can be fulfilled in a relationship with God. But, human nature looks to worldly relationships and temporary possessions for fulfillment. This creates hatred, turmoil and despair in people's lives. Although the abundant life is just a prayer of humility and repentance away, if considered at all, it is usually as a last resort.

Today, we watch the world struggle with hopelessness and despair. Society is trying to turn this destructive tide by promoting self-esteem, yet, this is nothing more than pride. Since pride is the main force behind the demand for rights without regard for others, the problem grows.

Many ministers have tried to solve this problem by encouraging their congregations to love themselves. The Bible already tells us that man loves himself. In fact, he cares for "self" religiously. The problem is that he hates his existence. This existence is not determined by how he feels about himself, but by what is happening in his relationship with others. By promoting self love, are we not also appealing to man's pride?

In studying the Jewish Orthodox culture, I discovered some interesting statistics. This subcultural society is not plagued with abortions, suicides or crime. To understand the main reason for the success of this culture, one must examine the code by which they live, the Ten Commandments.

We know the first four commandments lay a foundation for a right relationship with God. However, the last six commandments deal with our relationship with others. According to scholars, the number six represents the rebellion of man. We can therefore conclude that the last six commandments are a means of contending with rebellion in our lives.

We must ask, "what is the main theme of these commandments?" It is simple: respecting and maintaining the rights of others. In order to accomplish such a feat, we must prefer the other individual over self. By showing this type of preference, we are declaring that the other person has value and worth. By respecting the rights and dignity of others, we are establishing our own worth. This sense of worth will determine our attitudes. These attitudes will define the type of relationship we have with others; which defines the quality of our life.

Quality of life decreases when individuals or cultures undervalue life. For instance, if we consider the life of an unborn child to be non-essential, that lack of value affects our own existence. I believe we are seeing the results reflected in increased suicides, crime, hopelessness and fear throughout America.

It is obvious that pride in any form is not the solution. The Apostle Paul confirmed this truth by stating in 2 Timothy 2:11 & 12, *"that in order to have life, we must die and before we can reign with Jesus, we must suffer with Him."* Jesus summarized this principle when He gave the first command to his disciples, *"Deny self and pick up your cross and follow Me."*

Christianity involves the way of the cross. The cross is designed to deal with the issue of pride. Self must be sacrificed on a daily basis in order for Christ to reign as Lord and this is contrary to human nature. Christ is the example of a poured out life. As a result, the way of the cross is not an option for His followers. Obedience to the work of the cross is a must.

Once self is out of the way, basic needs are fulfilled and an abundant life is obtained. This is the result of having a right relationship with God.

As self is removed from the place of exultation, God is able to reveal Jesus Christ to us in a greater way. As we mature in our relationship with our Creator, the mind of Christ is worked within us. The result is the fruit of the Spirit.

In revealing the work of the cross to me, the Holy Spirit showed me a picture of the cross based on Matthew 5 and the four major relationships we are called to establish with our God. He showed me how the Beattitudes correspond with the four relationships. Consider the diagram on page 47.

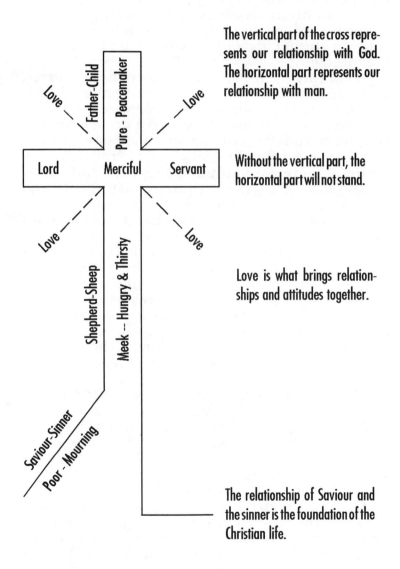

The vertical part of the cross represents our relationship with God. The horizontal part represents our relationship with man.

Without the vertical part, the horizontal part will not stand.

Love is what brings relationships and attitudes together.

The relationship of Saviour and the sinner is the foundation of the Christian life.

The **Foundation** of Christianity begins when we recognize our spiritual poverty. Because our sinful condition makes us poor in spirit, we begin to mourn. Mourning leads us to our Savior where we gain eternal life and are comforted because we are forgiven.

Maturing in Christ requires that a person come under the leadership of our **Shepherd**. This step implies becoming meek or manageable under the direction of Jesus. As we give up our right to self, we become more child-like and begin to hunger and thirst for the things of God. This new spiritual hunger and thirst is met on a daily basis as we submit to the scriptural instruction and direction of our Precious Shepherd.

Service is the result of Jesus becoming Lord of our life. A life of service comes from mercy, and mercy is the only spiritual ingredient that allows the Christian life to operate in the correct way. Because of mercy we can turn the other cheek or go the extra mile for an enemy. Mercy has no limit to its tolerance for other's actions and can only respond in humility when persecuted. But, mercy only functions when self is no longer there to take offense for abuse which will inevitably come to any servant of God.

Jesus died so we might have an abundant life. This complete life means we are abiding in the vine, Jesus, and have an intimate relationship with the Father. This intimacy means we will be at peace with God. Because of this peace we are able to help others enter into a relationship with the Creator, therefore earning the title of peacemakers. Matthew 5:11 declares that, *"the peacemakers shall be called the children of God."*

By the time we reach this stage, self is gone and we are able to identify with Christ in His sufferings. Persecution and tribulation will come, but those who have a right relationship with God will be able to trust in the Rock and endure to the end.

(Matthew 5:3-12; John 15:1-7; 1 Corinthians 3:16; 2 Corinthians 5:20; Ephesians 1:3-14 note verse 6-KJV; 2:13 & 14; 1 Peter 1:7 & 8; 2:4 & 5)

8

Pride in Action

Submitting to the flesh is so natural. Giving into pride and allowing it to reign is so logical. However, the flesh and pride must be crucified in order to ensure God's presence in our life. As we understand the makeup of human nature, we can appreciate the true plight of man.

It is vital to recognize pride in our own life. This occurs only when we understand how our own pride works, and begin to view its destructive devices from God's perspective.

There are three forms of pride found among the four natures: Conceit, selfishness and pride itself. These forms of pride have different attitudes, approaches and methods of preservation.

Conceit is a form of pride which enslaves the intellect. Our intellect determines our perception of what is important.

For instance, Proverbs 26:12 and Romans 12:16 say that intellectual pride makes a man appear wise in his own eyes. Proverbs 18:12 and 28:11 tells how the rich man's perception (or conceit) about his world of wealth makes him vulnerable. Jesus confirmed this when he stated that it was easier for a camel to go through the eye of a needle than for a rich man to enter the kingdom of God.

Conceit focuses on a person's attention on self. In other words, the person depends on an inward evaluation based on personal knowledge and perception instead of God. This brings us to the instruction in 2 Corinthians 10:5 which states, *"We demolish arguments and every pretension that sets itself up against the knowledge of God, and we take captive every thought to make it obedient to Christ."*

Conceit lacks confidence outside of the comfort zones it establishes for itself. If it begins to feel uncertain or unrecognized, it will ask for people's attention. This attempt to get people's consideration can be obnoxious and irritating. These irritations discredit the individual by making them appear foolish instead of wise; and to appear foolish implies failure. The fear of failure is the frailty conceit strives to avoid.

Selfishness is associated with words such as self-indulgence, vanity, ego and worldliness. This form of pride is defined by the outside world. It looks outward for its existence. It has an insatiable appetite which covets everything it values. According to Colossians 3:5 covetousness (or greed) is idolatry. As we consider self-indulgence, we can see the flesh taking precedence over God's will. In the case of vanity, the outward is being lifted above God's eternal perspective. In the area of the ego, self is being exalted above God's authority. As for having attachments to the world it's all vanity according to Ecclesiastes.

Worldly associations make us enemies of our Creator. Since the world is temporary, any pleasure one might experience from it quickly passes.

Selfishness totally emphasizes self. People who are driven by insatiable selfish desires can be very frustrating. As a result, they may be rejected. Rejection is the very reaction selfish pride fears the most.

This explains Solomon's answer and conclusion regarding selfish pride, in Ecclesiastes 12:13, *"Fear God and keep his commandments, for this is the whole duty of man."*

Pride is simply the exaltation of self and is described as idolatry in 1 Samuel 15:23. This particular form of pride encompasses the individual's inward world and the external environment. For instance, the inward world of self must be protected at all cost; and the outward environment must be controlled in order to receive both recognition and adoration from others.

This form of pride appears harsh, insensitive and unruly. It refuses to admit wrong and expects everyone else to agree.

Pride demands homage from its victims, and seeks to control others through intimidation. When confronted, or overlooked, it becomes offended. When offended, it mourns and pities the "poor mistreated self."

This type of pride fears two circumstances. The first is losing control of both worlds, and the second is appearing confused, incompetent and foolish to others.

By considering all three forms of pride we see how accurately Scripture points it out to us. Pride sacrifices the individual who allows it to rule. It not only causes them to feel ashamed because of failure, incompetence, rejection or loss of control, but it sets the person up for destruction.

The Character of Pride

Pride has a subtle nature. It compromises the truth, sacrifices people to maintain its position, and opposes God's nature.

Because of its ability to deceive, pride is one of our greatest enemies. Christians find that their real battle with pride takes place on the battleground of their faith. Jude 3 therefore, instructs believers, *"to contend for their faith."*

The reason that our faith is so important is that our identity rests in who God is, not on our idea of self. Exodus 20:5 tells us our *"God is a jealous God."* He refuses to adjust or bow down to our pride.

The more confidence we put in pride, the more the reality of God will elude us. As pride grows in power, God removes His presence from us. The more self is exalted, the greater the fall.

In contending with Christians who have fallen victim to this cunning culprit, I have been able to observe its unmerciful bondage. Once a Christian becomes aware of their pride, it breaks them; but then in a crafty move pride crops up in another form known as self-righteousness.

People trapped in self-righteous behavior punish themselves for belonging to the fallen human race and not being super spiritual. After flogging themselves, they express false humility and confess their error with the intention of showing how spiritual they have become in spite of their great sin. This continuous cycle ends in complete shame. However, many Christians do fall prey because they cannot accept the reality of their spiritual condition. Oh yes, they will agree that

they came to Christ as a sinner, but pride sh
be a thing of the past. The Bible's warnings a
the devices of the fallen nature can only be appl
to individuals who are considered less spiritu
than they. The instruction to *apply the cross daily* i
Luke 9:23 is simply a spiritual cliché to quote, not
an indication of an ongoing problem which must
be dealt with daily in their own life.

Here we see the clever disguises of pride.
Worldly repentance, false humility, martyr syndrome and self-pity are nothing more than masks
to cover man's true depravity. Self is exalted in
each case. People in these cycles set themselves
above all humanity. When they fall, it appears so
great that they cannot perceive that God's forgiveness is available to them.

How do Christians confront pride in their
own life? First, they must <u>recognize</u> it with the
intention of repenting before God. Secondly, they
must <u>confess</u> it to God. Thirdly, they must ask God
to give them His <u>perspective</u> of their pride. This
perspective should produce the fourth step, developing a <u>hatred for</u> it. No sin is overcome until a
perfect hatred for it is established.

The fifth step is to overcome pride. God
does take us through a process to bring us to a
place of truly being overcomers. The process is
rough and it reaches deep into our heart. In my
situation it was like having a suction cup applied to
my conceit. As God began to exert pressure, it felt
like everything was being pulled out of me. I stood
there knowing a big part of me no longer remained.
To be honest I was not sure I was still alive.

As time went by I felt God doing more work.
I did not understand the extent of it until one day
I became aware of an anchor. This anchor somehow held me steady in spite of all of pride's
temptations.

I questioned God about this steadiness. In
a gentle way He showed me the anchor replacing
the spot where pride so cleverly reigned. The

ingredient was simple, but profound. We know it as <u>sobriety</u>. Sobriety indicates one has mastered his/her own character. The truth is we never master anything, only God is capable of such a feat. Therefore, spiritual sobriety means God has subdued the root enemy of man.

Sobriety is made up of two godly virtues: fear of God, and humility. The fear of God is the beginning of wisdom. It is pure and hates all evil. It leads to salvation, compassion and protection. This attitude challenges vain imaginations, wrong motives, illuminates all deception and keeps us accountable to God's standard of holiness.

Humility means pride's independence, power and prestige has been crushed, allowing for submission and meekness to be worked into a person's character. When considering Jesus' character, we see humility. Although He could have exalted Himself, He chose a life of servitude and submission to the cross.

Sobriety gives us an eternal perspective. It keeps us on track with God's character. It enables us to be overcomers. Do you have pride or sobriety? If you have pride, allow God to break the control of pride and fill you with sobriety. Do not fool yourself by accepting fake humility. Test yourself. If you are not anchored, you do not have sobriety. Give God permission to work this ingredient into your life and be an overcomer.

(Psalms 19:9; 85:9; 103:13; 111:10; Proverbs 3:7; 8:13; 11:2; 16:18; 29:23; Matthew 11:28-30; 19:23 & 24; Philippians 2:5-9; 1 Thessalonians 5:6 & 8; James 4:6-10; 1 John 2:17)

Part Two
The Natures

9

Introduction to the Natures

The first question Christians need to ask is, "Is this information truly from God?" If it is, we as followers of Christ must allow the Holy Spirit to impart it into our spirits to bring forth fruit.

The spiritual test includes three considerations:

1) Does it call people to repentance?
2) Does it lift the Jesus of the Bible up as the only solution and source?
3) And, does it produce godly fruits?

This information was revealed to me when I asked God, "Why do some people go through extreme situations while others appear as if they hardly encounter any difficulties?" He showed me that people go through different processes. Some go through the process of a pearl, that is, irritations make them stumble. Others go through a gold process, either by sifting or boiling to bring separation. Some go through a diamond process, extreme heat and pressure to cause them to lose control.

The Word of God eludes to our process when it refers to trials and tribulations. God showed me later how these different processes are actually determined by how a person rebels against Him. These processes are designed to call us to repentance, submission and separation from self which results in maturity.

The fruits can be weighed as well. Our experience shows that this material has challenged and stopped destructive cycles in individual lives and relationships. It has given people greater understanding of themselves and others. It has set people free. It has helped parents contend with their children effectively and has served as a valuable key in ministering the life of Jesus to hurting and lost people.

Since each nature has different needs and walls of mistrust, you must approach the person based on their nature. By understanding a nature's need you will be able to communicate with the individual. This communication must be present in order for the individual to trust you with themselves. Trust will keep their wall down, and allow you to enter into this person's world, giving you the opportunity to minister the life of Christ to them.

The contrary happens when you do not understand what the different natures need. By not communicating their need based on their nature, you will encounter their wall of mistrust. This wall is a way of saying you do not understand me, therefore I cannot trust you.

Like Lady Godiva and her famous ride, sharing deep feelings, wounds and hurts can be dangerous. Although she put her clothes on after making her historic statement, people never forgot what they saw her do. Today she is known more for what she did, than for her cause. This is true of sharing our innermost being. People never forget what they learn about us. By opening ourselves up we could be giving individuals ammunition which may later be used to destroy us.

This information also allows us to accept ourselves. With acceptance, we can afford to acknowledge our weaknesses and understand our fears. Such acknowledgment implies we can become accountable for the way we respond and think. Accountability inspired by integrity produces repentance.

We will also know our strengths and the importance of them being under the control of God. This discipline is necessary to ensure that our strengths will become powerful in God instead of being used by Satan to destroy us.

We can allow ourselves to be vulnerable in ministry. Vulnerability involves suffering with Christ. The Apostle Paul declared, *"I want to know Christ and the power of his resurrection and the fellowship of sharing in his sufferings, becoming like him in his death."* This fellowship will make Christ our rock and confidence.

Acceptance is also vital if we are going to be receptive to others. Since we cannot change a person's nature, we must be willing to accept others just the way they are. Receiving people in this manner allows us to give them a break. Giving a person a break is a must in order to ensure trusting relationships.

God's Timing

We have had people say, "I wish I knew this information years ago. I would have approached problems differently with my spouse and children."

Jeannette and I have asked ourselves, "Why did God choose this time to illuminate these truths?" We both feel the Lord has a good reason for showing us this material now.

As never before God's people are searching for answers that will help them understand themselves and others. Christian Book Stores are full of psychology and self-help books. Seminars on developing healthy relationships are continually offered in churches.

Christians know Christ is the solution, but in their frantic search to get a handle on problems, it appears as if Christ is unable to deliver them from personal situations. We must ask our selves is Christ really able to liberate me from bad situations? If so, why am I not being an overcomer in these different problems?

The truth is many Christians can accept God intervening on behalf of others, but not on their own behalf. After all, why would God deliver them? This doubt towards God is nothing but a lack of faith--people simply do not believe God. His Word and promises are for the next guy and not for them.

All unbelief causes bondage. We therefore, cannot receive from God. Instead of recognizing that it is a matter of reaching up in order for God to reach down, we try to earn His approval through good works, worldly sorrow or penance.

This unbelief has created many blemishes and wrinkles among God's people. Remember what Paul declared in Ephesians 5, Christ is coming back for a church without "*spot and wrinkle.*" In order to fit this category, the church must be set free from destructive cycles, hurts and sins in order for the life of Christ to be worked out in the lives of believers. As the sinless life of Christ comes forth, believers will begin to overcome in His power and authority.

This material helps people to understand what they must overcome and how. It allows them to get a glimpse of Christ in light of the potential which can be obtained only in Him. In essence, this information is one of the tools of the Holy Spirit to prepare Christ's church for His coming. But like the gospel, it was a hidden nugget until God's timing brought it forth.

Much like the seed of the gospel which takes root in the heart of man, this information was formed in obscurity. It was refined by the harsh challenges inspired by a world which rejects and persecutes the things of God. It was buffeted by Satan and established in the fiery trials of faith. Finally, it has been confirmed and honored by the presence of God when presented, and verified by the evidence of godly fruit and liberty from all bondage.

Christ did come to heal the broken heart, set the captive free, give sight to the spiritually blind and hearing to the spiritually deaf. Our hope is in Him. But to realize our hope, our nature must come under the control of the Spirit. Our life must become hidden in Christ, the real cleft of our spiritual, unmovable rock.

The Three C's

The quality of meekness needs to be worked into each nature. This state means the individual has come under the control of the Spirit. This control means becoming manageable or flexible as clay under the sensitive hands or our great Potter.

By understanding the traits of our nature, we will know which traits must be <u>confronted</u> with the intent to <u>discipline</u> them. We will be able to recognize the characteristics we must <u>challenge</u> in order to <u>mortify</u> them. Finally, we must allow the Holy Spirit to <u>channel</u> traits in order to bring <u>glory</u> to God.

The traits which must be disciplined are those inspired by our soul. For instance, our thought process, emotions, desires, and standards must be disciplined in order to have correct beliefs. Paul talks about, *"bringing his body into subjection so he would not be a castaway."* He instructs us, *"not to yield our members as instruments of unrighteousness."* In Colossians three, we are told, *"to put on a new mind."* Philippians 2:5 instructs us to have, *"the mind of Christ,"* which will give us a correct perception.

We must put to death anything which demands obedience and homage. Paul makes reference to, *"mortifying whatever belongs to our earthly nature,"* in Colossians 3:5. In Galatians 2:20 he talked about, *"being crucified with Christ in order for the life of Christ to manifest in his life."*

One of the greatest traits we must put to death is our pride. Pride is intertwined with the very essence of our being. We must never let it reign, but there is a major battle which must take place in order to subdue its power in our life.

By disciplining traits and mortifying the power behind the fallen nature, we will be able to come under the control of the Spirit who will sanctify us. This sanctification will put our priorities, thought patterns and lifestyles in line with the holiness of God. An individual who is under the leading of the Spirit is what we call a <u>balanced person</u>.

Remember sin perverts the traits of man, but once those traits are under the power of the Holy Spirit they bring glory to God. This means a person's relationship with God has been restored. It is in an intimate relationship with the Father that people reach their potential in Christ.

If a person's beliefs are not inspired by the mind of Christ, they can become an <u>unbalanced individual</u>. Such an individual is focused on self and has an unbalanced perspective. This perception can serve as a door for Satan to enter in and push this person to the <u>extreme</u>.

Operating in the extreme simply means that people's traits are abnormal because of Satan's influence. This category includes those who are destructive not only to themselves, but to others.

So far we have identified three deceptive levels, three forms of rebellion, control and pride. People have three basic needs and desires. Traits of each nature must be confronted, challenged and channeled. All traits must come under the control of God, some must be disciplined while others mortified. Depending upon a person's beliefs or perceptions, their nature will be balanced, unbalanced or extreme. The number three means entirety or complete—in other words, we have a complete picture of rebellion, pride, needs and types of these natures. Let's summarize these different pictures.

Simple Picture of Human Nature

Deceptive Levels	Rebellion Levels	Needs	Desires	Forms of Control
Deal	Withdraw	Acceptance	Love	Words
Handle	Justify	Love	Peace	Attitudes
Take Care	Make Right	Recognition	Joy Happiness	Actions

Simple Picture of Pride

Conceit	Selfishness	Pride	Disguises
Asks for notice	Wants notice	Damands notice	Fake nobility & victims
Focuses on self	Emphasizes self	Preoccupied with self	Pity party

Categories of Natures

Balanced	Unbalanced	Extreme
Under God	Focused on Self	Influenced by Satan

Three Processes

Process	Three C's	Goals
Pearl	Confrontation	Disciplined
Gold	Challenged	Mortified
Diamond	Channeled	Controlled by God

There are four natures. In God's order the number four has to do with the function of the world. For example, there are four seasons, four directions, four elements, four natural laws, four types of flesh, four cups at Passover, four gospels, etc. If you add the number of natures with the three processes, you have the number seven. Seven is the number for perfection or maturity. This is God's desire for each nature.

God gave me the names of these four natures. The name of the nature is not a description of the person's character per se, but pertains to what we refer to as the "wall of mistrust."

Each nature has a different "wall of mistrust." This is the invisible wall of protection we put up to keep people who lack understanding of our need from coming in when we feel vulnerable. Although this wall serves as a means of protection from emotional damage inflicted by other people, it stifles valuable communication and keeps God from ministering to us. Therefore, we refer to this wall as a wall of rebellion.

This brings us to the identification of the four natures. They are:

Submissive
Stubborn
Self-Assured
Strong-Willed

Note, they all begin with the letter "s" so does sin, self and Satan. However, we must not forget our Saviour, salvation and sanctification also begin with "s." In order for each of us to overcome sin, self and Satan, we must receive the salvation of Christ and allow the Holy Spirit to sanctify our spirit, soul and body. By submitting to the process of sanctification in our life, we will be brought to perfection or maturity in Christ.

Understanding human nature as outlined in this teaching enables people to better understand each other. With this in mind, let's begin to study these different natures.

10

Submissive Nature

A submissive person will quickly <u>submit</u> to their wall of rebellion. Their wall is <u>fear</u>. This individual fears <u>failure</u> the most, therefore they strive hard to succeed. Any indication of inefficiency is taken personally, and if not confronted correctly, can end in complacency.

The way a submissive individual avoids failure is by <u>withdrawing</u> in order to <u>analyze</u> the situation and problem. In fact, their mind works like a computer.

As they confront each incident, they put it into a compartment with the intent of <u>dealing</u> with it after gaining the necessary insight to ensure success. Eventually all their compartments become full. Once this occurs, any added challenge will cause this person to explode. Since this nature is basically <u>sweet</u>, this emotional explosion makes them unmanageable and they will appear <u>obnoxious</u> to those around them.

I must state that the submissive person can never predict this outburst. The reason for this is because they are very <u>persevering</u> in their pursuits. This perseverance causes this individual to concentrate on what is before them, making them somewhat oblivious to what is happening around them. In a way, it can be compared to being surrounded much like an irritating grain of sand in an oyster which eventually comes forth as a <u>pearl</u>.

The submissive nature will first consider all their options. Once they select an option, they carry it out <u>methodically</u>. Since they are methodical, they have a set pace at which they can comfortably function. This pace can be slow, medium or fast. If you attempt to pressure them to go faster than their comfortable velocity, you will have a frustrated submissive person on your hands. This frustration can inspire the wall of fear to raise up, making them appear stubborn or strong-willed.

When dealing with a submissive person, give them the necessary time to feel at ease with new situations. Once they make peace with something different, they will continue on with any new challenge.

These individuals control with <u>words</u>. Since they only operate within a comfort zone, they will abstain from making any statements in unexpected confrontations. They will first withdraw and consider the incident and then they will devise a wise statement for a future encounter. These statements have a tendency to put people in their proper place.

Submissive people can appear <u>snobbish</u>. This occurs when the individual is not sure of what to say to someone. This uncertainty makes the submissive person mentally scramble for the right words. By the time they feel at ease with their declaration, they have already allowed the "moment" to slip by them. This can be true even in saying "hello" to someone. According to Proverbs, silence shows more wisdom. Therefore, a submissive person can rest better knowing their silence makes them appear wise, even though they are being classified as snobs.

These individuals not only hide behind walls of fear, they can retreat behind barricades of <u>eating disorders, alcoholism, drug abuse,</u> and <u>imaginary physical problems</u>. These excessive behaviors have three possible sources. First, they can be used to gain some semblance of control over their life. Second, they can be used to get attention; and third, they can be a means of self-punishment.

These behaviors focus the individual on themselves. If the focus is not redirected to Christ, it can lead to extreme and destructive behavior.

Pride in Action

Submissive people are motivated by <u>conceit</u>. It is important to understand that this person does not have any real image or idea of self. They are often referred to as having low or no self-esteem. They take pride in what they know and what they can do.

This conceit basically translates into intellectual pride and requires that the individual know the reasons and mechanics behind all ideas and concepts. This can cause the individual to over-analyze. It is at this point that, like all pride, conceit sets this individual up for a fall. For example, if the right conclusion eludes them over a long period of time, they can feel like a failure and become frustrated. This frustration can turn into complacency which serves as a "legitimate" excuse for doing nothing. Nothing equals zero and zero implies a nobody or a failure, the very state of being this individual fears the most.

Another area in which conceit sets this person up for a fall is how other people respond to this form of pride. People who encounter this pride become <u>irritated</u> with its methods of asking for attention.

Submissive people are afraid of being noticed, but they still desire recognition. This desire can eventually make them stand out obnoxiously, or it paralyzes them to such an extent they have difficulty having simple conversations with others. The outward appearance of conceit totally turn others off; the paralysis makes the individual appear whimpish or foolish resulting in the loss of respect.

Conceit disguises itself in the form of <u>false humility</u> or worldly sorrow. This individual can be very hard and unforgiving towards their "failures." They can whip themselves mentally or do penance by depriving themselves of the best. This subtle disguise only impresses the submissive person who is buying the deception of the sin of pride. Like all pride, this false humility is letting the individual "off the hook." Although they are taking some accountability for their "so-called" unforgivable deed, they are falling short of actually taking the <u>responsibility</u> for the real culprit behind their action--a prideful attitude.

The attitude behind fake humility is a dangerous game of the mind and ultimately calls God a liar. It declares God's grace is not sufficient in their particular case. It exalts the person above the rest of humanity by claiming the individual was too good to fall in the first place; therefore, they are not allowed to come to the cross seeking God's forgiveness and intervention like "the next guy."

The end product of fake humility is delusion. This delusion can result in the person operating in the extreme, resulting in self destruction. Self destruction means Satan managed to convince one more person to abide by his terms and he has the last laugh.

A submissive person who is being controlled by their conceit needs to quickly repent. This means coming to the cross and receiving God's forgiveness. It entails pushing past the game playing and the fear of accepting God's grace by faith. Remember, what is not of faith, is sin.

Overcoming

Like all natures, the submissive person must recognize the traits that need to be disciplined or put to death on a daily basis. This means they have to confront destructive and controlling characteristics with the determination to overcome. They must then challenge these traits by taking authority over them with the help of the Holy Spirit. Once these traits are subdued they can be channeled by the Spirit to bring glory to God.

The main trait which must be <u>disciplined</u> is their analytical mind. This individual will make molehills into gigantic mountains which will emotionally overwhelm them. If they consistently over-analyze a problem or situation, they will create mental ruts which can make them appear ineffective and sound like a broken record.

The fastest way for a submissive person to discipline their mind is by asking God for His <u>perspective</u>. God's perspective ensures balance in the life of a submissive person.

The two characteristics which must be mortified are the wall of fear and the conceit. Of course, conceit and fear walk hand in hand. The submissive person must overcome fear to allow God to reign in their life. They must allow their

71

conceit to be replaced with God's wisdom. God's wisdom is pure and can be described with two words: Jesus Christ.

The traits which must be channeled are their form of rebellion and their approach. Submissive people must make it a habit to withdraw into God to gain His perspective. They must become sanctified in their life before Him.

Once these traits are confronted correctly the submissive person will make God their confidence and rock. When God becomes their assurance, they become immovable pillars for the glory of God.

Confrontation

It is easy to determine when a submissive person is in their cycle. There are two indicators. The initial sign of the existence of a cycle are bad attitudes. Submissive people do not have strong attitudes per se; therefore evidence of bad attitudes imply there is a problem and action should be taken to avoid any possible extreme behavior.

Extreme behavior is the second indicator of a cycle. The problem with any extremity in the submissive nature implies they could be at the end of their cycle. The end of the cycle spells self-destruction. Therefore, it is easier to confront them, as with any nature, as they enter their cycle.

The main thrust behind confronting a submissive person is to challenge their perspective. In order to effectively do this, avoid being emotional or harsh. Since this individual plays emotional games, they do not respect emotional ploys. Respect is vital in all effective confrontation.

If you are too harsh, they will withdraw behind their wall. The least threatening way of confrontation is to firmly challenge the individual with facts. Once confronted, step back and give them space to consider what has been presented.

Now keep in mind a submissive person can be obnoxious in confrontation, but do not let that deter you from challenging their perspective. Once they withdraw with the facts, they will eventually get things in perspective. A submissive person will usually admit when they have been out of line.

(Romans 14:23)

11

Stubborn
Nature

A stubborn person's greatest battle is with their <u>emotions</u>. Although each nature has emotions, they come out at different points in their behavioral patterns. For the stubborn person, emotion is the first trait you will encounter. It is as though they "wear their feelings on their sleeves."

These emotions serve as the stimulant behind all the other traits of the stubborn nature. For example, they are <u>personable</u>. These people need to have interaction with others and are fun to be around. They can be very witty, but this outgoing personality may hide feelings of insecurity.

75

The stubborn nature's feelings make them impulsive. They can be impulsive in their decisions and in all their projects. In fact, they are persistent in their approach and have a very fast pace because they usually have many enterprises planned for the day.

Since these people feel very deeply about things, they can display fierce loyalty to causes, beliefs and people. Needless to say, misdirected loyalty can destroy this individual.

Stubborn people have a sense of fairness. This standard of fair play can get them involved in various causes. These causes can take them on detours and require much time and energy. Eventually, they are overwhelmed by their many projects and become very frustrated. This frustration is an indicator that this individual is now in their emotional cycle.

This emotional cycle starts when the stubborn person's plans are interrupted. They hate interrupted plans because it means they are not emotionally on top of the situation. The pressure begins to build, followed by frustration. Frustration is made evident by verbal complaining. Complaining is the process of justification which can be verified by strong attitudes of disapproval.

If the stubborn individual does not get the required response, the next response will be anger. This anger can be explosive. Once anger errupts, everyone involved with the stubborn person becomes upset. This anger serves as a release for the stubborn person's emotions, but the disturbance they cause can remain with those who encounter this explosive passion.

The next step in the emotional pattern of the stubborn person is guilt. Although the stubborn person feels justified in their anger, doubt begins to invade their conscience. This doubt brings guilt which is quickly reinforced by Satan.

Satan starts to support this guilt with condemnation. Condemnation produces fear of rejection. Since the stubborn person needs emotional love, fear of rejection leads them to the final destination of their emotional pattern which is depression.

A stubborn person strives hard to earn love for two reasons. The first has to do with being needed. These people need to feel needed in order to sense purpose in their lives. They need to have a reason for getting up to face every new day. They try to fulfill this need by doing many deeds to make themselves indispensable to their family and employers.

The second reason for earning love is because they require proof of love. Stubborn people tend to be gullible. This gullibility is based on their innocent desire to be transparent with others in the hope they will be loved for themselves. Once they realize people are taking advantage of them, they become judgmental.

Their judgmentalism is based on standards. Although these individuals hate being boxed in, they will box God and everyone else in with their standards. If not challenged, these standards can be unmerciful. As these standards exalt the stubborn person to a superior position, they can become harsh and very skeptical about anything which does not quickly line up with their feelings or standards.

Once a stubborn person reaches the stage of skepticism, Satan is indeed on the scene. Satan will use their rebellious wall of stubbornness to strengthen their rigid standards. The stubbornness becomes an immovable idol and the standards, the stubborn person's final authority.

A stubborn person is a survivor, but if they resolve to settle for a bad situation they can give up their identity. When this happens they become a zombie.

When Pride Hits the Scene

Pride is the last trait which makes its entrance on the scene with the stubborn nature. The form of pride which motivates a stubborn person is selfishness. This selfishness comes out after the stubborn individual has attempted to earn love without any success.

Once the stubborn person feels unappreciated, they become frustrated. This frustration is verbally expressed. As the emotional momentum builds, so does the appetite of selfishness as it starts to emphasize self. This appetite becomes insatiable and causes frustration for those who are trying to satisfy it.

Feelings of being used surface in the stubborn person and can be translated into betrayal. These emotions create the martyr syndrome.

As a martyr, the stubborn person becomes a suffering, silent victim. They feel that people should recognize their plight and enter in emotionally with them. Often they are ignored, which is perceived as rejection. This rejection implies they are not loved. The end of this cycle can be depression or self-destruction.

Selfishness also creates a paradox. Stubborn people are very giving, but the generosity is inspired by their selfishness. Ultimately, they must be number one. They want people to exalt them in order to feel needed, understood and important.

Overcoming

Stubborn people must discipline their emotions. Many times these individuals seek emotional fulfillment in fleshly pursuits including: drug and alcohol abuse, sporadic shopping sprees and all forms of entertainment. In fact, this nature equates their deep feelings with intellectual superiority. After all, how could anyone really understand the depth they have experienced in their soul?

The stubborn individual can team up with "underdogs." Their emotional level can cloud the real motivation behind their commitments to these types of people. In the end the "underdogs" may succeed in dragging down the stubborn person, therefore, they need to keep loyalties in perspective.

It is vital that a stubborn person tests everything by the Word of God. Emotions or feelings are not a sound gauge to determine truth. In fact, they will lead you far from God's will and perspective.

Also in the area of emotions the stubborn nature must be aware of their need to sense God's love. If a stubborn person does not feel God's love, they decide that He does not love them. We walk by faith and not by sight or feelings. Stubborn people need to exercise faith one step at a time, and not by their feelings.

Stubborn people must avoid taking everything personally. They can over react to situations or read rejection into people's unemotional responses. These over-reactions can be related to exaggeration.

A stubborn person must put to death their selfishness. This selfishness does have an insatiable appetite. The desires to ultimately control others to ensure order in their environment is generally unsuccessful. This lack of control results in frustration and causes division in relationships.

The stubborn person must put down their standards. These standards can serve as unmerciful judges. No matter how religious or righteous these standards may seem, they must never become as the final authority. Check out attitude and motivation. If the attitude is judgmental, repent.

Remember, all things are to be done in love and we must have the mind of Christ in order to accomplished this goal. Christ's attitude is one of humility, meekness and compassion. Check the fruit which is coming out of your life.

The stubborn nature must be <u>separated</u> from their ability to quickly justify their decisions and actions. The problem with this justification is that it can become a con game. The Holy Spirit uses ongoing friction to <u>sift</u> this individual. It appears as if sparks and friction surround the stubborn person most of the time.

People who are stubborn by nature have to put their fear, guilt and doubt in <u>perspective</u>. They must cease to care what other people think about them and focus on God's will in situations. The problem with caring about what others think is that this concern creates a bondage. We end up putting more stock in what people are thinking than in coming to terms with God's mind about a situation. Jesus came to set us free from all such bondage.

In the areas of guilt and doubt, God's forgiveness and love will put these emotions in the right aspect. The stubborn person must get beyond their emotions to accept both God's love and forgiveness by faith.

Stubborn people must <u>channel</u> their stubbornness. This stubbornness must come under the control of the Holy Spirit. The Holy Spirit will turn the direction of their stubbornness from personal causes to God. Instead of being stubborn about what is important to them, they will become stubborn about the things of God. Stubbornness which is properly focused is an asset and not a liability.

Other areas which are reinforced by stubbornness such as persistence and loyalty, must also be channeled by the Holy Spirit. Since the stubborn person can be emotionally inconsistent, they must become persistent in establishing a right relationship with God. Their loyalty must be given to Jesus Christ, and once this loyalty is correct, Christ can put other relationships and priorities in a right perspective.

Confrontation

Stubborn people do have a distinct pattern eluded to in the first part of this chapter. The pattern begins with interrupted plans. Emotional pressure begins to build. Frustration follows and is reinforced by complaints. These complaints are verbal expressions of the justification which is being done in the mind. The next stage in this pattern is explosive anger, followed by guilt and condemnation. It all ends in emotional depression.

Stubborn people need to take the initiative in challenging this pattern but it must be done in the early stages. The best place to confront this pattern is at the point of frustration. Once the stubborn person feels pressure and frustration because of interrupted plans, they must stop and contend with their emotions.

Jeannette, who is stubborn by nature puts her emotional plight in perspective by asking herself a simple question. It goes like this, "Will it matter a hundred years from now if I cannot accomplish all that I have planned for today?"

It is important to understand where a stubborn person is in their pattern in order to effectively confront them. The stubborn person must be challenged in their early stages to avoid encountering the full impact of their emotional momentum.

Once their momentum is built up, these people have a tendency to run over anyone who might confront them.

Remember, they have to be challenged at the point of their frustration, but in order to do it effectively you must enter in with them emotionally. If they don't feel you are joining them in their plight, their wall of mistrust will spring up with an emotional vendetta. By acknowledging their frustration, hurts or insecurities, their wall of mistrust stays down and you can challenge them sucessfully and help them avoid their emotional spiral into depression.

(Proverbs 29:25; Luke 4:18)

12

Self-Assured Nature

The self-assured person has one main trait they must overcome: <u>pride</u>. This nature is the only one of the four that has an <u>image</u> <u>of</u> <u>self</u>. This image is like putting on the mask and costume of a popular character and acting this personality out twenty-four hours a day, seven days a week.

This individual in fact, has various images. These images change with the individual's positions or responsibilities. For example, if a self-assured person is a spouse, parent, employee, etc., they have separate images for each responsibility. They actually change hats for each role.

83

Occasionally conflict arises when they must live up to more than one image at a time. To avoid conflict, these individuals prioritize their images. If their desire is to be known as the best parent, then their role as spouse will be sacrificed to maintain the desired image of parent.

This image is based on the self-assured person's perception. For instance, it is not unusual for the male gender of this nature to appear "cool" or "macho" to those around them. This "cool" or "macho" image is based on the "images" produced for TV, advertising, and movies. This individual observes and interprets behavior from childhood and begins to try to live out their acquired identity.

Their idea of self becomes the motivation behind attitudes and responses. The self-assured person, for example is <u>unpredictable</u>. They avoid making decisions because if they are wrong, their image will be shattered. In order to maintain their image, the self-assured nature will offer "logical" choices and expect others to make the decisions. The acceptable choice can be narrowed down further by a display of <u>strong</u> <u>attitudes</u> of either approval or disapproval.

The self-assured nature is <u>reserved</u>. This means you will not be allowed to go very far into their mind or heart. This inability to be transparent is the result of their fragile images. Let's consider for a moment that this individual may sense they are not really what they claim to be. If they fall short of their image, it will be translated as <u>incompetence</u>. This individual fears incompetence and may become neurotic wondering how others perceive them.

The self-assured individual has a <u>lawyer's mind</u>. They actually keep a <u>list</u> of everything bad that has happened to them. In confrontations, the self-assured person uses their list to <u>justify</u>, condemn and pronounce judgment on the "so-called" culprit. The list also supports a <u>reservoir</u> <u>of anger</u> which produces harsh judgment.

This harsh judgment can result in acts of violence, sexual deviation and verbal cruelty without any show of remorse or conscience. These types of <u>actions</u> occur because the self-assured's image was not <u>recognized</u>. Therefore, the self-assured person has a right to accumulate condemning evidence against those who failed to give proper homage.

A self-assured person is very <u>inventive</u> and <u>meticulous</u> about doing projects. They determine projects according to whether they can carry them through successfully, although some self-assured people are considered procrastinators who rarely finish any project. This is especially true on the home front. In order for self-assured people to exhibit <u>persistency</u> in their endeavors, they must see the end result of any enterprise and it must maintain and comply with the image they are trying to portray.

The self-assured nature has two walls of rebellion. These walls are used to protect their image. The first wall is <u>stubbornness</u>. This stubborn wall displays much emotion, but the emotions are often inspired by <u>self</u> pity. These emotions are also used as a means to control others. In fact, a self-assured person may be a suave con who can delude and sweep people off their feet by portraying a "<u>good guy</u>" image.

The second wall of rebellion is <u>pride</u>. This pride serves as an immovable wall. This wall is harsh and <u>unyielding</u>. It refuses to submit to any challenges or concerns. This wall ensures that the image will be protected at other people's expense.

A self-assured woman confirmed the need to protect self from any vulnerability. She related how she watched her father victimize her mother while growing up. She did not respect her father, but at the same time she was not about to become defenseless like her mother. She eventually found herself actually siding with her father.

The self-assured person constantly finds themselves juggling or even changing their images. At times they find they are experiencing total <u>confusion</u> especially when reality challenges their image. Other times they appear to be walking a fine line between sanity and insanity. One minute they can appear confident about themselves and the next moment be totally bewildered about their identity. If this individual gives up trying to appease their image, this cycle may end in apathy.

Individuals who are self-assured by nature are greatly <u>influenced by their childhood</u>. Ideas of self are formed and reinforced by childhood images. These images are accumulated through observation of people they respect. For this reason, parents need to identify their child's nature in order to effectively challenge them.

Overcoming the Image

The advantage in being self-assured is, they only have to put down their image in order to win! In fact, they must totally separate themself from their images in order to receive the image God desires for them. God actually separates them from their images through the <u>boiling process</u>, much like what <u>gold</u> goes through when it is being refined.

This boiling process may include long term illnesses or situations which tear at the heart of the self-assured person's perception of self. The process may almost destroy them. But, the self-assured person must let God have his way with them. In order to let God be God they must <u>mortify</u> their image. This is a wrestling match much like Jacob's recorded in the book of Genesis.

Jacob, which means deceiver or supplanter, wrestled all night long with a heavenly being after being boiled in the midst of deception for twenty years. After his encounter with the heavenly being, he came out Israel, prince of God. Keep in mind, Jacob came out with the image God designed for Him before the foundation of the world.

For the self-assured person to be happy they must have the image God intends. They must allow destructive, self-righteous and controlling attitudes to be exchanged for godly attitudes and standards. They must get rid of their list in order to empty their reservoir of anger and cease from being an unmerciful judge.

Self-assured people need to be aware of their destructive behavioral <u>patterns</u>. These patterns usually start with strong attitudes. They must become accountable for any wrong attitudes and actions by quickly bringing them under the control of God and seeking His perspective.

People who are self-assured by nature must beware of <u>doublemindedness</u>. These people must see purpose and direction in order to have commitment. Doublemindedness and confusion are the result of the self-assured person being fragmented in their commitments. This nature must therefore, insure singlemindedness by knowing God's will and purpose for their life.

A self-assured person must not give in to <u>self-pity</u>. Self-pity implies that an individual has the right to feel sorry for themselves because they have not had due recognition. Such recognition brings the self-assured person into competition with God. Personal luxury of this type must be avoided.

Confronting the Images

People who are contending with this nature must <u>recognize</u> that images do exist. Confrontation should never be based on the person, but on the image the self-assured person is portraying. This image must be treated with respect. I must state you might not appreciate or agree with the image, but you must acknowledge its existence.

In confrontation with a self-assured nature, refrain from <u>arguing</u> with them. You will never win any argument. Regardless of the facts, you will come out confused and victimized. Keep in mind that such encounters are a means of justification for this nature, and allows them to gain control.

Avoid, at all costs, reacting to a self-assured person's attitudes, excuses and self-pity. These are means of entrapping and controlling others. Strong <u>attitudes</u> mean the self-assured person is in their cycle. The most predominate attitude is anger. Anger instills fear and intimidates others.

<u>Excuses</u> are nothing more than ways to justify wrong actions. A self-assured person is very clever at justifying. They can eventually convince those around them that they are the guilty party. Therefore, never attempt to defend yourself as you may end up feeling guilty.

Do not respond to a self-assured person's self-pity. These people can be very emotional, especially when they are not getting their way or their covert misdeeds have been discovered. These people want you to enter in with them emotionally and help make their life better. This means either you will become a scapegoat or you must become a god who orchestrates every activity to ensure the self-assured person's well-being. Of course, the latter is impossible, so the sacrifice of the scapegoat is the remaining choice.

Ultimately, you must call this person to <u>accountability</u>. I remember when a self-assured husband was upset about his wife's family not showing up at the time he had calculated. He began to put pressure on his wife by displaying strong attitudes. He backed up these attitudes with verbal, unmerciful criticism. The wife began to feel the heat and frustration. She finally realized if she could change the situation to please her husband she would, but then again she was not God. She looked at him and in a decisive manner informed him she was not God and that he had to contend with his own attitudes and opinions. The facts challenged him and he apologized in an indirect way.

Self-assured people do not necessarily realize what they are doing to others. They can be pretty self-centered. Self of course, gives them a narrow perspective of what is going on around them. This narrow perspective causes their harsh response to others which ultimately makes them appear foolish and unreasonable.

(Genesis 25:24-32:28; Ephesians 1:4)

13

Strong-Willed
Nature

The most challenging trait for a strong-willed nature to contend with is their need to <u>control</u>. This individual controls in three areas: through atmosphere, decisions and intimidation.

The strong-willed individual has an air about them. This air has been incorrectly referred to as attitude. Attitude comes from within while air stipulates the <u>atmosphere</u> around a person. In some cases you can walk into a strong-willed person's home or office and get a definite sense of the individual's identity and what they expect from you. In an indirect way you find yourself reacting to the unspoken expectation of this person's atmosphere.

Strong-willed individuals are people of <u>action</u> which serve as their means of control. Their actions are based on unseen boundaries which determine their <u>decisions</u>. These decisions are based on what these people consider to be the <u>facts</u>. These facts are sometimes founded on past experience or gut-level feelings. This combination gives the strong-willed person confidence to carry out their decisions because they feel they have come to the right conclusion.

Their decisions serve as a <u>decisive</u> judge of matters and beliefs. You usually never have to guess what this individual thinks. The strong-willed person actually <u>draws</u> their own conclusion about what is right or wrong and these conclusions establish lines or boundaries. Because they draw their own conclusions, ultimately they become <u>right in their own eyes</u>.

This ability to adjust ideas to their conclusion presents the strong-willed individual as <u>dynamic</u> or forceful, which usually enables them to become successful in their endeavors. This forcefulness <u>intimidates</u> others around them. People find themselves adapting to the decisions and ideas of the strong-willed person without fully understanding why.

The strong-willed person is <u>extreme</u>. They can be extremely quiet or extremely personable. They can exhibit excessiveness in their atmosphere. For example, a strong-willed person can be very neat and selective about the objects in their home or they can go to the other extreme. Regardless of the extremes they know exactly what is in their valued space and strive hard to maintain control.

This intensity follows the strong-willed person into their emotional make-up. Although they can appear quite calm on the exterior, much is going on in their mind and emotions. They strive hard to control not only all emotions, but their atmosphere as well. Their <u>greatest</u> <u>fear</u> <u>is</u> <u>losing</u> <u>control</u>.

A strong-willed person who is out of control feels vulnerable. This can create explosive anger or emotional outbursts. During such times, you may have an opportunity to minister to them.

Their wall of rebellion is comprised of all the traits of their <u>nature</u>. The combination of their traits gives them a <u>feeling</u> <u>of</u> <u>infallibility</u>. Strong-willed people seem to have the ability to control not only their emotions, but their situations. Since they have this ability, this individual can appear fearless about dangerous situations or new horizons.

A strong-willed person may seem narrow-minded. They can be hard towards those who oppose them or who show emotion. They can display harsh control and demands on those around them or they can act totally oblivious to everyone and everything. Once again, extremity can be identified in this nature.

Strong-willed people can be motivated by <u>any</u> <u>of</u> <u>the</u> <u>three</u> <u>forms</u> <u>of</u> <u>pride</u>. Some are conceited, some are selfish and some have pride. Since this nature is so decisive, you never have to guess what form of pride motivates a strong-willed individual.

Forms of pride, decisions and priorities will determine this person's position and response in their relationships. For instance, if two strong-willed people pair off, their forms of pride could determine which one will be more dominating. Selfishness overrules conceit and pride is more confident than selfishness.

Their decisions are another influencing element in relationships. A strong-willed husband may decide to pamper his wife. This pampering may create an unbalanced wife. A strong-willed wife may decide to become submissive to an unbalanced husband and loose total perspective as to what is really going on in their relationship.

Overcoming

A strong-willed person must <u>discipline their conclusions</u> (or what makes them right in their own eyes). This discipline takes place when the strong-willed individual ensures that their conclusions about right and wrong lines up with God's standards of holiness. A strong-willed lady shared with me how she asked God to show her her conclusions. He did. She found out her conclusions ran parallel with His standard of holiness, but did not align with His will.

It is vital that strong-willed people examine their conclusions based on the Word of God and also test their spirit and motivation. They must always ask themselves, "Why do I insist on maintaining my conclusion? Is it because it is God's will or am I trying to be the final authority in this situation?"

Strong-willed people must <u>mortify their need to control or rule</u>. Control outside of the Holy Spirit is rebellion against God. It is an act of witchcraft. The strong-willed person must therefore become manageable or meek under the power and rule of the Spirit. This meekness will ensure their openness to wise counseling and instruction.

Strong-willed people should surround themselves with wise counselors. Counselors and openness are two allies which may help this nature avoid going through their extreme process. The process this individual goes through is that of a <u>diamond</u>.

A diamond begins as a piece of coal which goes through extreme heat and pressure. It is in the midst of this process that the coal takes on a different structure and appearance. But heat and pressure are not enough; a diamond must be cut to make it more valuable.

Strong-willed people can find themselves almost being consumed by intense circumstances. These drastic situations sometimes occur because the strong-willed person was not sensitive to the warnings or problems that pressed around them. Eventually the strong-willed individual hits an immovable wall. This always shocks them and can result in an extensive emotional pity party.

It is in the middle of these trials that a strong-willed person loses control. Their conclusions and boundaries are challenged and their self-confidence (pride) is shaken. Tremendous fears and insecurities surface to add to their plight. At this time they must make a decision--look to God or try to regain control of the situation. If they look to God, they must <u>know</u> <u>they</u> <u>are</u> <u>not</u> <u>infallible</u> and put their <u>pride</u> <u>to</u> <u>death</u>. If they look to self, God will intensify the process by turning up the heat and pressure.

Strong-willed people need to know that even after the process of heat and pressure, God will continue to cut and polish them. Strong-willed Apostle Paul was reduced from a religious Pharisee to the chief of sinners. In the book of Philippians, Paul counted his prestige, education and material possessions as dung. He learned to put self down so that he could gain Christ, who was his real hope of glory.

Confronting the Diamond

It is important that you have the <u>respect</u> of a strong-willed person in any confrontation. The strong-willed person only respects people who respect them. I must state that fear or intimidation is never interpreted as a show of respect by the strong-willed individual.

To understand the correct respect, you must keep in mind that this person is a diamond. Diamonds are regarded as valuable in our society. You do not handle this valuable gem lightly. This is true of a strong-willed person. Never respond to them in a light manner. <u>Look</u> <u>them</u> <u>in</u> <u>the</u> <u>eyes</u>. This is the way you communicate respect to them.

In confronting a strong-willed person, <u>avoid emotions</u>. Strong-willed people feel emotions cloud the issues. These people want the <u>facts</u>.

When presenting facts to them, be clear and decisive. Keep in mind this individual will draw their own conclusion, so do not try to prove your position. Once the facts have been stated, back off and let them make up their mind.

It is important to remember that a strong-willed person may not agree with your facts. Do not take it personally. This individual has their own standards of right and wrong and will draw their own conclusions based on their boundaries.

(Philippians 3:4-14; Colossians 1:27; 1 Timothy 1:15)

In Review

Let us now compare the differences of these four natures. It is obvious they have different processes, rebellion levels, responses, personalities, forms of pride and walls of rebellion. Consider the chart on page 97. The differences are simple, yet they are far reaching when it comes to how each nature responds in crises and in their relationship to God and others.

TRAITS	Submissive	Stubborn	Self Assured	Strong Willed
PROCESS	Pearl	Gold	Gold	Diamond
REBELLION	Withdraw	Justify	Justify	Make Right
RESPONSES	Analytical	Impulsive	Un-predictable	Decisive
CHARACTER	Sweet	Personable	Reserved	Extreme
CONTROL	Words	Words Attitudes	Attitudes Actions	Actions
APPROACH	Persevere	Persistent	Persistent	Dynamic
PRIDE	Conceit	Selfishness	Pride	Any of the Three Forms of Pride
WALL	Fear	Stubborn	Stubbornness Pride	Nature
NEED	Acceptance	Love	Recognition	Recognition

Part Three
Recognizing Our Potential in Christ

14

Accepting Our Place in Christ

As the Lord began to verify the nature information, the Holy Spirit illuminated the natures of men and women in Scripture. I started to see how these people had various leadership abilities and how God revealed Himself and dealt with them according to their nature.

I noticed that Christians of different natures had distinct positions in the church based on the strengths and weaknesses of their nature. They had diverse prayer lives and presented the things of God in a format which corresponded to their nature.

99

As these differences between the natures became obvious, the ramifications of this information became overwhelming. I have watched so many believers compare themselves with other Christians. They watch hopelessly from the sidelines because they want a prayer life like someone else, or have ability to gain understanding of Scripture like another believer.

I started to realize the secret to spiritual success is to recognize and accept both the weaknesses and strengths of our nature. A submissive person will not have the same leadership ability or position in the church as a strong-willed person. The Apostle Paul made reference to this fact in 1 Corinthians 12 when he stated that the body of Christ is made up of different parts, and each part is equally important and necessary for the church to function properly.

As this information developed, I became excited. I watched it set people free as they began to realize their importance and potential in the kingdom of God. Instead of feeling like outcasts, people started to get excited about their weaknesses becoming strengths for the glory of God, and their strengths becoming avenues in which He could reveal Himself to them.

The picture of these four natures functioning within the weaknesses and strengths took on greater meaning when God uncovered, to Jeannette, their importance in the church. (You can find Jeannette's explanation of what God showed her in chapter 16.) Each nature, when conformed to the image of Christ, depicts the complete image of our Precious Lord to the lost world. My, how the lost world needs to see the fullness and power of Christ in the church today!

To be conformed to the image of Christ involves a process. This process includes the two vital works done by the Word of God and the Holy

Spirit. These works are: sanctification and regeneration.

Sanctification is a work of separation for the glory of God. Regeneration is the new life coming forth.

These processes were made real to me when I was studying the offering up of Isaac by Abraham in Genesis 22. Abraham made a three day journey to Moriah to offer, not only his most precious son, but the promise God had given him about a nation coming from Isaac. This journey represents a separation. This separation for the Christian begins with the application of the cross to their life. They must offer their lives as a sacrifice. As they allow the cross to work, they will become separated from the world and from a worldly mindset in order to have the mind of Christ.

There were two types of offerings. One was a sin offering where the blood of the animal was sprinkled on the altar for the sin of man. The other was a burnt offering. This offering not only involved the offering up of a living sacrifice, but burning it as well. Frankincense was poured on the sacrifice in the rituals set up in the Tabernacle. Although the sacrifice was consumed by the fire, the fragrance ascended to heaven as a sweet savor to God.

Isaac was to be a burnt offering. Abraham not only was required to sacrifice him, but he had to burn his body as well. We know that this was a test of Abraham's faith, but we also know Isaac, Abraham's best, was not an acceptable sacrifice to God. In a way, Isaac was an example of a living sacrifice in which God fulfilled His promise to Abraham.

This powerful story points to the only acceptable sacrifice, Jesus Christ. As I considered the applications of this to my own spiritual life, I began to see an awesome picture of what it really means to reach our potential in Christ.

The first time Christ came, He came as a sin offering, but we also know He was a burnt offering. However, Scripture shows us that his body was not burned so how could he be a burnt offering?

The Holy Spirit reminded me that where Christ ended as the sin offering on the cross, His complete body, the church must continue on as a living sacrifice to fulfill God's plan on earth. As the fiery work of sanctification burns up the associations and residues of the world in His body, the life of Christ will come forth in power and beauty. This new life is the work of regeneration.

Ephesians 5:2 tells us that *"Christ gave himself out of love for us as a fragrant offering to God"*. In Second Corinthians 2:15 it tells Christians that they are *"the fragrance of Christ to both the saved and to those who are not saved"*. Do you see the picture? Christ becomes the complete (burnt) offering to both God and the world through His body, the church.

I realized that there was no real acceptable sacrifice I could give God. Like Abraham who offered his best, my best was as dirty rags before Him. It was my reasonable service to offer my life as a living sacrifice. As I pondered what possible sacrifice I could give God, I was reminded of Hebrews 13:15 & 16. There were two acceptable sacrifices I could give God: the sacrifice of praise and of giving to others.

The real test behind Abraham's journey and sacrifice was not the sacrifice of Isaac, but his faith in God. Christians are to walk by faith not by sight, therefore, real and acceptable praise can only come out of faith.

Faith

The reason faith plays a major part in genuine praise is because the acceptable sacrifice of praise will come forth in the midst of trials and tribulations. It is indeed hard to praise God when everything is going wrong, but faith is not determined by circumstances.

Real faith rests on who God is. We believe God and appropriate His promises because He is trustworthy and capable of fulfilling them. The Apostle Peter put it this way, *"Though you have not seen him, you love him; and even though you do not see him now, you believe in him and are filled with an inexpressible and glorious joy."* Jesus adds to this simple picture with this statement, *"I have told you this so that my joy may be in you and that your joy may be complete."* The joy comes out of knowing His purpose and plan for our lives.

Faith not only inspires the sacrifice of praise, but it results in doing good for others. James makes this truth clear in 2:18 when he said, *"But someone will say, 'You have faith; I have deeds.' Show me your faith without deeds, and I will show you my faith by what I do."*

In observing the different natures we can see where the strengths of each nature can <u>replace faith</u> and <u>hinder</u> true and acceptable praise. For example, the submissive person has a tendency to depend on their analytical mind over the wisdom and truth of God in order to understand the reason behind a situation. The stubborn person will allow their feelings and emotions to serve as their final authority rather than the Word of God. The self-assured person often tests themselves by their image rather than the fruit coming out of their life. The strong-willed people will put their trust in their conclusions rather than testing the spirit behind their actions. These strengths replace faith in God; therefore, they must be disciplined and brought under the control of the Holy Spirit. Once these strengths are under the control of God, He can begin to reveal Himself to them through these very same avenues. On the other hand, if these areas do not come under the control of the Spirit, they will actually reinforce independence or rebellion in each nature.

In 2 Corinthians 12:9 Jesus made this declaration to the Apostle Paul, *"My grace is sufficient for you, for my power is made perfect in weakness."* As each nature recognizes and brings their weaknesses under the control of the Holy Spirit, they will become strengths in the kingdom of God. As you will see, some of these weaknesses can be used to bring leadership qualities to the church of Jesus Christ.

In the next few chapters you will begin to discover your leadership abilities, and your position and potential in the kingdom of God. You will see how God ministers to each nature differently in their prayer closet, and how these natures under the control of the Spirit, represent God and His kingdom to a lost world.

(Isaiah 64:6; John 7:17; 15:11; Romans 12:1; 15:16; 2 Corinthians 5:7; Ephesians 5:26; Titus 3:5; 1 Peter 1:8)

15

Spiritual
Examples

Submissive Nature

One of the greatest prophets who was sub-missive by nature was Elijah. Elijah displayed great fear when hearing the threats of Queen Jezebel to kill him, but also showed unwavering faith on Mount Carmel when his <u>focus</u> was on his great God.

This is the real key behind spiritual authority for a submissive person. Their focus must be on God. A right focus ensures a correct perspective of God. An upright perspective produces child-like faith in a submissive person. This <u>child-</u>

like faith helps the submissive individual put their confidence in God, and not their analytical mind.

Daniel is a good example of a submissive person whose confidence rested in God. Daniel 1:8 gives us a clue to Daniel's faithful, obedient life before his God. The secret to Daniel's godly life was that he purposed in his heart to do it God's way.

Daniel's decision to obey enabled him to seek God in the midst of crises. Under the sentence of death as he interpreted King Nebuchadnezzar's dream, we see Daniel withdrawing to seek God's mind in the matter. In the lion's den we see Daniel standing in their midst, untouched, a spiritual pillar who rests securely on the rock of Jesus.

Submissive people who are resting securely on the rock, Jesus, serve as immovable pillars in the church. The submissive Apostle John was referred to as a pillar of the church in Galatians 2:9.

John was the apostle who laid his head on the chest of Jesus. This response gives us an insight into the sweet, sensitive heart of a submissive person. This sensitive heart can be tuned in to God's Spirit, and obedient in response. Such a heart is representative of a servant's heart. According to Matthew 20:25-28, *the greatest in the kingdom of God is a servant to all.* Therefore, a godly submissive individual serves as an example of the truest form of leadership in the kingdom of God.

Submission is considered a weakness in our society. However in the kingdom of heaven, it holds both strength and power in God's purpose and plan for His people. Submissive people must realize the strength of submission is found in quickly submitting to their God out of fear of who He is, rather than submitting to their wall of fear. God is trustworthy and deserves our obedience and our undivided respect and loyalty.

In order for the heart of the submissive person to line up to the authority of the Holy Spirit, their mind must come under the control of the Spirit. Submissive people must discipline their mind. They must bring into captivity every thought and plan. Ultimately, they must have the mind of Christ to reach their potential in Him.

The mind of Christ can only be established in a submissive person as they allow the Spirit to surround them with God's perspective and life. Like the pearl which takes on the complexion of the one who wears it, the submissive person will begin to reflect God. Their heart will be sensitive to the Holy Spirit. They will have a mind which displays submission before God and humility towards others. They will live an obedient life before the lost.

The life of Christ reigning in the submissive person will bring balance to their life. The submissive person must be balanced in order to function properly in the kingdom. The Apostle John gave insight to a balanced perspective in Revelation 1:1. His perspective was the actual revelation of Jesus Christ.

Isaiah who was submissive by nature gave this insight into his perspective, *"In the year that King Uzziah died, I saw the Lord seated on a throne, high and exalted and the train of his robe filled the temple."* What a perspective! What a vision! It's no wonder a submissive person has the capacity to reflect the beauty, sweetness and pureness of their God.

God entrusts a submissive person with much in His kingdom. Consider Isaiah, Daniel and John who were given detailed prophecies about the end days and the Millennium. Isaiah's writing is considered the miniature Bible. John's writings reveal Jesus as the Son of God and as the Truth. The submissive handmaiden, Mary was entrusted with the Son of God; and the Apostle John was honored at the cross when Jesus asked him to take care of His mother.

107

The prophet Elijah was entrusted with much as a prophet. He was one of only two people in the Bible who did not see death, but was translated. He made a second appearance on the Mount of Transfiguration with Jesus and the great lawgiver, Moses. Many Bible Scholars believe Elijah will make a third appearance during the time of great tribulation in Revelation 11.

In his first adventure here, Elijah called the leadership of Israel back to God. In his second visit, he called attention to the One, (Jesus the focus of all Bible prophecy). If he is one of the witnesses in Revelation 11, he will challenge the people of Israel to acknowledge and accept their Messiah who was crucified and rejected 2,000 years ago. He will become a relentless thorn in the side of the Gentile world. In considering Elijah's first and possibly third appearances, I could see how his second sighting on the Mount of Transfiguration could be brought into sharper focus. Jesus is the one who is the true Messiah and Savior of all of Israel and the world. Elijah, a submissive person, was entrusted with the greatest perspective of all, a revelation of our only hope of glory. Today, submissive people have the opportunity of revealing the hope and glory of Christ Jesus in us.

(1 Kings 17-21; 2 Kings 1-2; Isaiah 6; Daniel 2:14-30; 6; Matthew 17; Luke 1:26-33, 2:26-56; John 13:23; 19:25-27)

Stubborn Nature

One of the most popular stubborn people of the New Testament was the impulsive Peter. Peter has been held up as an example of what a person should avoid in their Christian walk. He has been criticized for sinking in the water after taking his eyes off of Jesus. However, few ever acknowledged that out of the twelve men in the boat, Peter was the only one who got out of the boat to walk on the water.

Many remember how Peter denied Christ at the crucifixion, but few point out how all the other disciples totally deserted Jesus at the very beginning. We have to at least credit Peter with being in the same vicinity as Christ during his trials.

Few ever expound on Peter's accomplishments. For example, he was the first of the disciples to declare Jesus to be "the Christ." He was the first disciple at Jesus' empty tomb. He was the first one to preach the salvation message after the Holy Spirit fell on the 120 at Pentecost.

It is obvious that even in the kingdom of God, the stubborn person is often misunderstood and criticized. This, of course, is due to a stubborn person's emotional instability. One minute Peter was zealously defending Christ to the death and the next moment he denied Him. This instability results from a stubborn person trusting their deep feelings and not God. Likewise, this emotional weakness in the stubborn person serves as an avenue of greatness for God.

God changes their emotional weakness into a stable, unaltered leadership quality in the kingdom of heaven. God brings forth this powerful leadership in the stubborn person through proof.

Stubborn people seek this proof because they do not trust their decisions. This need for proof has brought much criticism from those who do not understand the stubborn person's insecurities. They do want to please God. God honors this desire by giving them the proof they need.

In the case of Gideon, God honored his two fleeces. In the incident of Thomas, Christ invited him to put his hand through His nail-pierced hands. In response to the imprisoned John the Baptist's inquiry about Jesus being "the Messiah," Jesus told John's disciples to tell him of the miracles He was performing. In Peter's situation Christ appeared to him in a personal way after His resurrection. Jesus later asks Peter three times to verify his love for Him and gave him a blueprint for his life. This blueprint must have brought security and stability to Peter. It showed him that in the end he would die for his Precious Lord.

After Peter's traumatic sifting process, we see him becoming Cephas, a small stone. Christ uses this small stone to preach the first message of salvation after the Holy Spirit fell in the upper room. Jesus actually added other stones (people) to Peter, the first visible stone, as He started building His church on the day of Pentecost. What a beautiful picture of the stable, immovable leadership the stubborn person can bring to the church if they are under the control of God.

Stubborn people can prove to be <u>powerful adversaries</u> to the kingdom of darkness. Like <u>Gideon</u>, <u>Joshua</u>, and <u>Nehemiah</u>, stubborn people have the potential of being mighty warriors. Joshua determined to serve God no matter what confronted him. Nehemiah stood with a sword in one hand while building the wall with the other hand. The key to the stubborn person becoming mighty in God is knowing and recognizing the real enemy.

Fears, guilt and condemnation often paralyzes the stubborn person. They spend much of their time wavering between doubt (fears) about their own spiritual condition and the guilt of constantly feeling responsible for all the problems occurring around them. This combination of fear and guilt leads to condemnation which is brought on by Satan.

Once the stubborn individual realizes that the real enemy is Satan, they can turn their fears, guilt and condemnation into righteous anger against Satan. This anger becomes a fire igniting the initiative to stand up and take authority over all enemies.

A stubborn person can be used as a plumb line in the church. In fact, they will plow up the fallow ground of a person's heart. Their sense of right and wrong is an avenue God uses to call them forth as prophets like Jeremiah and John the Baptist. Jeremiah called Israel back to their God and back to a life of separation. John the Baptist prepared the way for the light of the world, Jesus Christ. John came from the wilderness with authority, calling people to repentance and exposing the hypocrisy of the religious system which kept people from truly worshipping God.

The emotional sensitivity of a stubborn person can be a channel for God to give them insight into the spiritual realm. It is therefore, vital that stubborn people have their emotions under God's control. God desires to use their emotional sensitivity in the area of visions, dreams, prophecy and discerning of spirits. Satan on the other hand can use this same sensitivity to execute his power of witchcraft.

Stubborn people must not only guard their emotions, but their hearts as well. Stubborn people feel deeply about beliefs and convictions. Beliefs and convictions may be critical and harsh, or they may be means for God to use a stubborn person in a victorious way. This was obvious in the cases of Nehemiah and King David.

Nehemiah not only physically built the wall, but he contended with the Levites when it came time for them to separate themselves from their foreign wives and children. King David was able to defeat the giant, Goliath. Both men knew God was their defense. Both of them recognized their enemies. Ultimately, they were able to accomplish the feats God entrusted to them.

Scripture shows us the heart a stubborn person must have to reach their potential in God. King David is a good example. The Word states that David had a perfect heart. He followed God with his whole heart. David's heart actually inspired him to be a man after God's own heart. He was obedient to God. He was emotionally tuned into His God. This was made evident in the psalms he composed. These psalms not only expressed David's sensitive heart towards God, but they reveal God's majesty, His faithfulness to those who love Him and His unchanging glory. The psalms show us David knew his God!

The Word tells us David walked according to the integrity of his heart. This was made real when David was confronted by the prophet Nathan over his sin with Bathsheba. David had the honesty to take responsibility for his actions. We see him acknowledging the real implications behind his sin in Psalm 51:4, *"Against you, you only, have I sinned and done what is evil in your sight, so that you are proved right when you speak and justified when you judge."*

Stubbornness controlled by and directed towards God is a powerful trait. This stubbornness was displayed by both Joshua and Mary Magdalene.

Joshua did not let the fear of the ten spies deter him from wanting to enter the promised land. In the end, Joshua was entrusted with leading the nation of Israel into the promised land.

Mary Magdalene did not allow the events of the crucifixion and the disciples' fear to keep her away from the tomb. As a result, Mary was the first one to proclaim the resurrection of Christ.

It is easy to see how stubborn people under the control of the Spirit bring a bold and stable leadership to the kingdom of heaven. They are powerful soldiers who can put the enemy on the run. Once these people are pointed in the right direction they will plow up the fallow ground of people's hearts, they will call the sinner to accountability, and they will be the first on the scene to fight the battle and become the ultimate sacrifice. It is because of such authority and willingness, that

God can entrust His kingdom to their sturdy leadership. They are indeed capable and trustworthy.

(Numbers 13 & 14; Deuteronomy 34:9; Joshua 1; 24:15; Judges 6 & 7; 1 Samuel 17; 1 Kings 3:14; 9:4; 11:4 14:8; Nehemiah; Jeremiah; Matthew 3:1-12; 11:1-6; 14:22-33; 16:13-16; 26:69-75; Mark 1:1-8; Luke 24:33-36; John 20:2-4; 20:24-29; 21; 26: 35, 69-75; Acts 2)

Self-Assured Nature

Self-assured people have the potential to see into the spiritual realm, but for a different reason than a stubborn person. Stubborn people must see in the spiritual realm for a blueprint of what is happening and proof of God's approval. Self-assured people must see in the spiritual realm for purpose and direction, and then they must have proof God is capable of bringing forth His promises. This became obvious in the lives of Jacob and Moses.

Jacob met God at Bethel. He witnessed the angels ascending and descending from earth to heaven on a ladder. God introduced Himself to Jacob and passed on the promise He had given previously to Abraham and Isaac. He promised to bring Jacob back to the land He had given his forefathers. The next morning Jacob made a vow to God. The vow was simple. He made a commitment to make Him the God of his life if He would provide for him and bring him back to the land. Twenty years later God fulfilled his promise. He brought Jacob back to the land with family, animals and untold riches. God had kept his end of the bargain and now Jacob keeps his vow by making God the Lord, his God.

God showed Moses that he was to lead the people of Israel out of Egypt to the promised land.

God confirmed His promise in the burning bush, gave Moses a rod of power, and sent Aaron to assist Moses. Once God silenced all of Moses' excuses, we see Moses making the trip to Egypt. God's miracles proved to Moses that He is true to His word. The end result of God's proof is that Moses finally becomes the committed leader of Israel.

Commitment brings out the leadership of strength which has been stifled by the images of a self-assured person. The self-assured person must know why they are exchanging their images. In the cases of Moses and Jacob, it was the promised land. However one must keep in mind, that Jacob spent 20 years at the mercy of his unscrupulous uncle Laban, and Moses spent 40 years in the wilderness as a mere shepherd. What a boiling process for both men!

In order for Jacob to replace his image, he first had to overcome his old image. His image was defined by his very name, Jacob, the deceiver and supplanter. Overcoming this image involved a wrestling match with a heavenly being. This wrestling match was no small matter. It was an all night battle.

In Jude 3, we are told to 'contend or wrestle for the faith." Jacob was really wrestling with his old self in order to place his faith in God and not his image. After all how can God be Lord of anybody's life if they do not have faith in Him? Jacob came out of the wrestling match with both a curse and a blessing which gave him a new identity in God.

The curse was a thigh out of joint. This could be considered a thorn in Jacob's side. Paul said his thorn, "kept him from being exalted above the Lord." An interesting way for God to contend with Jacob's pride and keep him humble before Him. Jacob's own words reflect humility when he declared, "I am unworthy of all the kindness and faithfulness you have shown your servant."

The blessing Jacob received came in the form of a new name--Israel. Jacob no longer was a deceiver or a supplanter, but now he was a Prince of God. What a contrast. A deceiver is considered despicable, but a prince is royalty and in line to rule. Jacob now knew his position. As prince he would bless the very Pharaoh of Egypt. However he would never supplant the authority of the only One who was in leadership over him, the King of kings, the Lord of lords, the Creator of the universe and God Almighty.

Let us now consider Moses. He spent his first forty years in a prestigious position at Pharaoh's court, then finds himself in the wilderness tending sheep after killing an Egyptian. What a demotion. Moses who was in line to be an Egyptian ruler is now a shepherd, an occupation considered an abomination by the Egyptian culture.

By the time God appeared to Moses in the burning bush, He had dealt with his pride. Moses' fears, insecurities and excuses give ample evidence of this fact. God managed in time to replace Moses' bumbling image with the one He intended for him all along.

God took his fear and put authority in its place. He took his lowly shepherd's staff and gave him a rod of power. He took his ineloquent speech and replaced it with a decisive voice that rang in the courts of Pharaoh. He substituted the nation of Israel for his sheep. He replaced Moses' indecisiveness about circumcising his sons with a commitment to write, proclaim and teach the law of God which would help circumcise hearts.

Moses' flight from Egypt started after he defended one Israelite, but 40 years later he interceded on behalf of the entire Nation of Israel in the very wilderness where he found refuge. During his intercession, God offered to make him a great nation. This meant the destruction of the children of Israel. Instead of accepting God's offer he offered his own life in place of the nation of Israel. Does this sound familiar?

✕ Who came as a shepherd with power and authority? Whose voice has sounded down through the corridors of time and given warnings which rang out in the synagogues? Who not only taught the law, but fulfilled it? Who serves as the living Word that not only circumcised hearts with truth, but as the Rock, has the capacity to break the proud heart? Who gave up the glories of heaven to come to earth to die on an old rugged cross on our behalf?

Moses is a type of Christ. God actually conformed Moses to the image of Christ. We know that after his mountain top experience, Moses' face radiated the glory of God. He had to put a veil over this beautiful radiance. II Corinthians 3:13, 15, 16 & 18 states, "*We are not like Moses, who would put a veil over his face to keep the Israelites from gazing at it while the radiance was fading away. Even to this day when Moses is read, a veil covers their (Israel) hearts. But whenever anyone turns to the Lord, the veil is taken away. And we, who with unveiled faces all reflect the Lord's glory,...*" Colossians 1:27 goes one step further to define this glory, "*...Christ in you, the hope of glory.*"

Moses was entrusted with much as a leader. God showed him many great things and as a result, Moses was held more accountable for his actions. In an angry fit, Moses struck the rock, which represented Christ, twice. As a result, he would never enter the promised land. Although he tried to blame the children of Israel for his angry reaction, in Deuteronomy 1:37 and 3:26, we see God holding him accountable for his own response in the wilderness in Deuteronomy 32:51-52.

The main ingredient to ensure victory for a self-assured person is to have a broken heart and a contrite spirit. We see the right heart condition and the right attitude in the lives of these men. In Bethel, Jacob developed a fear of God when he witnessed the heavenly ladder. Moses had a repentant spirit after his forty years in the wilderness. In the case of a man named Job, we see a real regression of self, ending with brokenness and a revelation of a holy God.

Job's statements give us insight into his commitment to God and his regression after his boiling process. Job 13:15 shows us that Job, above all, trusted God, *"Though he slay me, yet will I hope in him;..."* Job's next declaration revealed his uncompromising confidence in his Redeemer in 19:25 & 26, *"I know that my Redeemer lives, and that in the end he will stand upon the earth. And after my skin has been destroyed, yet in my flesh I will see God (my Redeemer);."* Job showed his totally yielded life and heavenly hope when he acknowledged God's process at work in Job 23:10, *"But he knows the way that I take; when he has tested me, I will come forth as gold."* In Job 40:4 and 42:5 & 6, we see Job's spiritual progression (actually regression of self) in his final responses to God, *"'I am unworthy--how can I reply to you? I put my hand over my mouth...My ears have heard of you but now my eyes have seen you. Therefore I despise myself and repent in dust and ashes.'"*

Job stood righteous before God, but when compared with God's holiness, he discovered the truth we read in Isaiah 64:6, *"All of us have become like one who is unclean, and all our righteous acts are like filthy rags; we all shrivel up like a leaf, and like the wind our sins sweep us away."*

Job's commitment to God made him upright, but the revelation of God's holiness made him acceptable. He was acceptable because he became broken and humbled before his Holy God. God will never resist a broken heart and a repentant spirit.

The self-assured person can only reach their potential when they forget about themselves (images). Then as with Moses, they have the ability to be a protector of God's holiness, law and His people, rather than compete with Him.

We see this same type of protection in the life of Sarah, Abraham's wife. Sarah's name was changed to fit her life into God's plan. Instead of being Sarai, my princess (Abraham's princess), she became "Princess," a woman who now belonged and became subject to God.

We see Sarah defending God's plan by demanding that Hagar and Ishmael be sent away. Ishmael's apparent disrespect for Sarah and her son implied future conflict. She knew God's promise was to come down through Isaac and there could be no challenge or competition. Her protection of what God had entrusted to her was unwavering. God ordered Abraham to obey her.

In order to avoid competing with God, self-assured people must allow God to break them at their point of pride, and exchange their images for His image. Of course, this exchange will never occur without a process. The problem is that most self-assured people refuse to lose their image. As a result, they go through extreme fires. Instead of repenting, they often yield to worldly sorrow and self-pity like King Saul. They avoid being accountable for their unyielding and harsh manner. Many times they prefer a delusion over the image God wants to give them.

Outward acceptable repentance can be seen in the life of King Ahab. However, Ahab's life shows that self-assured people's repentance must go below the surface (images) and become a matter of the heart.

We see unpredictable Ahab pouting over not getting his way concerning Naboth's vineyard. His spoiled attitude prompts his evil wife, Jezebel to plot against Naboth. Naboth loses his life; then the prophet Elijah enters the scene.

Elijah pronounces judgment upon Ahab and his household. 1 Kings 21 tells us that upon hearing Elijah's words, Ahab tore his clothes, put on sackcloth, fasted and went around meekly. We read

God's response to his actions in 1 Kings 21:29, *"Have you noticed how Ahab has humbled himself before me? Because he has humbled himself, I will not bring this disaster in his day, but I will bring it on his house in the days of his son."*

What a change in direction, but not in commitment and determination. We see King Ahab up to his old tricks in 1 Kings 22. He prefers a lie over the truth. We see him protecting himself and being quick to sacrifice unsuspecting people (Jehoshaphat), but in the end he loses his life.

Ahab's selfish and destructive pattern is consistently found among self-assured people who refuse to be accountable for their attitudes and actions. We see God bringing all self-assured people to accountability from Adam and Cain to Jacob, Moses and Ahab. Self-assured people can be assured of one thing, God will make you accountable, no matter how you may justify all of your unfruitful acts.

Self-assured people must test themselves by the fruit coming out of their life and not by their deceiving images. They must be aware of fragmentation in their goals and purpose for God. They must take stock at any indication of confusion. They must be teachable, so godly warning and reproof will not fall to the way-side. They need to keep in mind that because God has intrusted them with much, they will be held accountable for much. They must remember that people should not have to pay homage to their attitudes and images in order to be heard. Proverbs 12:15 tells us *"The way of a fool seems right to him, but a wise man listens to advice."*

(Genesis 3:12, 17; 4:8-16; 17; 21; 27-50; Exodus 2-20; 32-34; Numbers 14; 1 Samuel 13-15; 18-31; Job 1:8; 2:3 & 10; Psalm 34:18; 2 Corinthians 12:1-10)

Strong-Willed Nature

There is always a disturbance when a strong-willed person enters the scene. We see this in the case of strong-willed individuals in the Bible such as Joseph, Jonah and the Apostle Paul. Joseph's attitude caused his brothers to despise him so much that they sold him into slavery. Jonah almost brought destruction to an unsuspecting ship crew. Paul wrought havoc with the new Christian Church.

A strong-willed person's decisive reactions enables them to bring decisive leadership to the kingdom of God. This powerful leadership must come under the rule or control of God. A strong-willed person whose leadership is not properly channeled by the Holy Spirit is not only dangerous to those around them but destructive to themselves.

We see this in the case of Jonah. Jonah decided not to obey the Lord's command to go to Nineveh. He jumped ship sailing in an opposite direction. God sent a great wind that almost sank the ship. Jonah finally confessed that he had displeased his God. The crew threw him overboard to save their own lives.

The key to strong-willed people being godly leaders rests with where their conclusions or boundaries of right and wrong are. It is amazing to watch the conclusions a strong-willed person will have concerning the things of God. These conclusions may totally line up with God or they can run closely parallel to His will. The problem with the latter is that it can look right and sound right, misses the mark of what is right to God. The Apostle Paul is a good example of totally missing God's will.

Paul saw the followers of Jesus Christ as enemies of God. He became the greatest foe of the new faith. He persecuted Christians with a fervent and relentless conviction. He knew without a doubt he was doing a service for God. He was truly sincere, but he was sincerely wrong.

Strong-willed people must, therefore, be aware of their conclusions. Ungodly conclusions can delude a strong-willed individual. We see this in the lives of Queen Jezebel and King Nebuchadnezzar.

Jezebel still chose to believe in her pagan god after witnessing the miracles performed by God through his prophet, Elijah. She tried to destroy Elijah. She already had led Israel into greater idolatry and killed innocent people for her own selfish gains. Her violent end was inspired by her own wicked deeds.

King Nebuchadnezzar had encountered the God of Daniel, Shadrach, Meshach, and Abednego in miraculous circumstances. The God of the Israelites had given Daniel a revelation of both the king's dream and its interpretation. God delivered the three Hebrew men untouched from the fiery furnace much to the king's amazement. Nebuchadnezzar had declared that the Jewish God was the God above all gods. In spite of his encounters with God Almighty, he still saw himself as the ultimate ruler. A year after being warned in a dream he found out who really ruled both the heavens and the earth. God brought a decisive judgment upon Nebuchadnezzar to break him. Unlike Jezebel, King Nebuchadnezzar did repent. We read this declaration from him in Daniel 4:37, "Now I, Nebuchadnezzar, _praise_ _and_ _exalt_ _and_ _glorify_ _the_ _King_ _of heaven,_ because everything he does is _right_ _and_ _all_ _his_ _ways_ _are just_. And those who walk in pride he is able to humble." What a complete change! He was now exalting God and not himself.

Ungodly boundaries require extreme measures on God's part to adjust strong-willed people to His nature, will and plan. These people find themselves in intensive situations. Joseph spent years in slavery and prison. Jonah was swallowed by a fish. Nebuchadnezzar spent seven years roaming around like an animal. Paul lost his sight on the road to Damascus. We see God taking all their control away from them. However, it is in the midst of their fiery process that these people's traits were brought under the control of God.

In Joseph and Nebuchadnezzar's case, their pride was replaced with humility. Jonah's right to determine what he would do for His God was replaced with a fear of God and the response of submission and obedience to Him. Paul's zealous conclusions were aligned to God's will, bringing forth meekness in his life.

This meekness is made evident throughout Paul's letters to the churches. Paul who reproved the apostles for trying to burden the Gentiles with circumcision, makes this statement in 1 Timothy 1:15, *"Here is a trustworthy saying that deserves full acceptance: Christ Jesus came into the world to save sinners--of whom I am the worst."*

Diamonds are not only formed in extreme heat and pressure, they are cut to make them more valuable. Paul was cut to form the special vessel God called him to be before the foundation of the world. His cutting process came through various persecution and trials.

Once a strong-willed person's conclusions are adjusted to God's will, they serve as great assets to the kingdom of God. Their leadership brings definite value to the kingdom of heaven. They can serve as wise judges and leaders like Deborah. Deborah victoriously lead the nation of Israel into battle. Joseph was used to save his household from famine. Jonah was used to spare the city of Nineveh from God's immediate judgment. The Apostle Paul opened the door of the kingdom of God to the Gentile world.

What value, what leadership! These qualities will only exist when strong-willed people have a singleness of heart. This singleness will inspire a strong-willed individual to serve God with all of their heart. They will decide to let God rule in each decision and situation.

(Genesis 37-50; Judges 4 & 5; 1 Kings 16:28 - ch.21; 2 Kings 9:30-37; Daniel 2 & 3; Acts 8 & 9; 2 Corinthians 11:23-33; Ephesians 6:5-7)

16

The Overcoming Church

Jesus commands and empowers His church to be overcomers. By gaining an understanding of our own nature and form of pride we can be set free through true repentance. At this point we as believers are challenged and called to scale the heights which God has divinely ordained for each nature.

Bear in mind that in the beginning our Creator God made man in the image, likeness and resemblance of Himself. The entire Creation, from the least to the greatest, all that exists both materially and spiritually and every written word which originated from the Spirit of God culminates in one great and glorious purpose -- to reveal and exalt the Lord Jesus Christ. This is the high calling of God in

125

Christ Jesus for all four natures within the church, the Body of Christ. All four natures together in one body are divinely commissioned to reflect, resemble and radiate the resurrected Christ to a lost and dying world.

Is the church today *"in all her glory, having no spot or wrinkle or any such thing;...holy and blameless?"* In these last days will she be prepared for the glorious appearing of the Lord Jesus Christ by overcoming the world, the flesh and the devil or of necessity must she be purified by persecution? The answer lies, hidden from human view, within the foreknowledge of God. But by His Spirit, our true Teacher, we are given an awesome vision of what you and I, the church of Jesus Christ, are summoned to be. And by understanding our God-given nature, we can acknowledge and accept the potential and position in His Body to which we are called.

Remember, all Scripture is for the purpose of revealing Jesus Christ. With this in mind, we examine two passages, Ezekiel 1:10 and Revelation 4:7, concerning four beasts, or types: the lion, the calf or ox, the man and the eagle. Then there are the four gospels, Matthew, Mark, Luke and John. And finally, the four natures, submissive, stubborn, self-assured and strong-willed.

It is the intent in the following pages of this chapter to explain the correlation between the gospels, the beasts (or living creatures) and the natures.

The Book of Matthew, the first gospel, is factual and decisive, written in a strong-willed manner. It portrays Jesus Christ as the King of kings and Lord of lords. He is the Lion of the Tribe of Judah. In Revelation 5:5, 6 we see the Apostle John beholding the Lion of the Tribe of Judah. And as he beheld the Lion, he saw instead the Lamb of God. Interestingly, the Lion of Judah is always depicted in conjunction with the lamb!

You who are strong-willed by nature are "li-ons" in the body of Christ. The lion is officially the "king of all the wild beasts." No one disputes his regal demeanor, power or control. With kingship come four distinct attributes -- authority, royalty, strength and power.

Because the Lion of Judah is presented in conjunction with the Lamb of God, we begin to see the secret to greatness within the kingdom of God. The strong-willed lion must become like a lamb-- gentle, humble, meek and submissive, in the fear of God.

How can the strong-willed person reflect Christ within the church? How does this nature exhibit the authority of God unpolluted by their nature's tendency to control? The answer is gentle-ness. *"You have given me the shield of your salvation: and your gentleness has made me great."* KJV Ps.18:35. In Strong's Concordance (SC), "great" means to increase; be in authority. The strong-willed Christian reflects God's authority within the church and to the world through the gentleness of Christ.

The second trait, royalty, means rule, domin-ion, sovereign, kingly, a foundation of power, (SC). True royalty in the kingdom of God is obtained by humility. We read that, *"blessed are the poor in spirit; for theirs is the kingdom of heaven."* KJV Within the church the need for recognition must be laid aside. Poor" means "beggar, cringing pauper." (SC) In other words, as the humility of Christ is worked into the strong-willed nature, all pride is crumpled into dust and laid at the Savior's feet.

The third characteristic is strength. Strength means fasten upon, seize, conquer, withstand, mighty, prevail, (SC). All natural characteristics of the strong-willed nature. But under the control of the Holy Spirit, this strength is exhibited to both the world and the church by true meekness. Re-member, *"blessed are the meek for they shall inherit the earth."* Inherit means to be an heir. We are joint-heirs with Jesus Christ. And this inheritance comes through total surrender to the risen Christ, not through our own ability to conquer or through the might of the flesh. True meekness is strength under control, the control of the Holy Spirit.

Finally the fourth attribute of kings and lions is power. The secret of displaying the power and glory of God is obedience through submission. God accomplishes His will, *"not by might, nor by power, but by His spirit."* Jesus is truly lifted up when members of the body of Christ submit one to another in the fear of God.

Strong-willed people, unless ruled by the Holy Spirit, are unruly. The key is the little root "rule." Who is in control, who is ruling? Is it the Holy Spirit? If you are strong-willed, are you unruly, drawing your own conclusions? If so, consider Jesus, who even though He was the King of kings, exchanged a crown for a cross.

The strong-willed Apostle Paul could confidently adjure the believers of his day to follow him as he followed Christ. Through his extreme process he had allowed himself to become a lamb, obediently and meekly following the Lion of Judah.

Strong-willed Christians are called to reflect the very attributes of God. But to do so, they must first sacrifice pride, and then lay it on the altar. The very thing which you desire most, (recognition), must be given to others. This is true kingship and leadership in the kingdom of God.

The second gospel, the book of Mark, depicts Jesus as the Servant, Burden Bearer and the Sacrifice acceptable to God. The symbol is the Ox, the king of all tame beasts, and the nature represented is stubborn.

The book of Mark is believed to have been dictated to Mark by the emotional and impulsive Peter. It is full of proof for those who either have never heard the good news or doubt its validity.

People who are stubborn by nature are usually misunderstood and very often sacrificed. Because of their honesty (or bluntness), they can "plow deeply" into people's lives. And because of persecution they can identify with the sufferings of Christ, our Supreme Sacrifice.

Romans 12:1 tells us to *"present our bodies as a living sacrifice, holy, acceptable to God, which is our reasonable service"*, KJV. This takes discipline. And the natural spirit of the stubborn nature is "undisciplined." This nature needs discipline in order to feel secure, but detests being "boxed in," "pushed," or brought under "control."

Some scholars believe that Hebrews 12:2, (*"looking unto Jesus, the author and finisher of our faith; who for the joy that was set before Him endured the cross, despising the shame, and is set down at the right hand of the throne of God"*), actually refers back to the Old Testament where the Levitical priests were required to examine each part of the sacrifice. The four things they examined and the spiritual applications are as follows:

First to be examined was the head of the sacrificial animal. The head represented the intelligence and the thoughts. Philippians 2:5 tells us to "Let this mind be in you, which was also in Christ Jesus." The stubborn individual must discipline their mind to become the mind of Christ. All "intelligence" must be brought under the control of the Holy Spirit.

The second portion to be examined by the priest was the fat. The fat represented the general health and vigor, or excellency of the sacrifice. How often we bring that which is not excellent to God. We offer a diseased and unacceptable offering when we give second-best in the name of the Lord. Giving that which costs us little or nothing is not an acceptable sacrifice to God! Beware of selfishness! Proverbs 11:25 tells us that the *"liberal soul shall be made fat: and he that waters shall be watered also himself"*. And Psalm 92:12-14 indicates that *"the righteous shall be fat and flourishing"*. Fat in this context means to anoint; to satisfy; to be rich, fertile, (SC #1879). In other words, bring the best to God and He will bring anointing, satisfaction, richness and fulfillment to your life.

Thirdly, the innards were examined because they represent the motives and affections. Remember, Colossians 3:1-2 reads: *"If you then be risen with Christ, seek those things which are above, where Christ sits on the right hand of God. Set your affection on things above, not on things on the earth."* Here again discipline must be exercised to "set" affections heavenward.

Finally, the priest examined the legs of the sacrificed animal. The legs represented the walk. 1 John 2:6 admonishes: *"He that says he abides in Him ought himself so to walk, even as He walked."* And how did Jesus walk? Always in the will of the Father. He walked a straight walk, not turning to the right or to the left. He walked in God's timing and God's way with God's anointing. He walked up Golgatha. He walked to the cross.

Stubborn people, how is your walk? Are you yoked with Christ? An ox begins his training from the very first day he is born. If left to roam around the pasture, they become difficult to discipline. Oxen do not respond to brutal treatment, but respond by vocal command. They do not require elaborate harnesses and bits like horses, but only a simple yoke.

Stubborn people love their freedom (much like wild horses), but God requires that they become a living sacrifice, yoked with His Beloved Son.

In the book of John, Chapter 21 verses 18 and 19 we read that Jesus told Peter he, *"would some day walk where he didn't want to walk."* Peter knew what kind of a death he would die. He was comforted by knowing that no matter how much his emotions fluctuated, no matter how much he failed, some day he would be a sacrifice acceptable to God.

In the church, the stubborn nature is the "heart" and the prophetic voice. By putting self-ishness to death on the altar, all the love this individual craves can be lavished on others.

The third gospel, the gospel of Luke is where we see Jesus portrayed as the Son of Man. Jesus, God in the Flesh. Obviously, the Man is represented in this gospel as well as the self-assured nature, for man was created in the image of God.

Hebrews 7:26 says, "For such a high priest became us, who is holy harmless, undefiled, separate from sinners, and made higher than the heavens." We see four things in this verse which describe Jesus, the Son of Man. Holy, harmless, undefiled and separate from sinners.

The Bible records four things about Job. He was: "perfect, upright, feared God and avoided evil." Because of these qualities, Job's image was that of his Creator. Little wonder Satan wanted Job to fall!

Perfect means complete, pious, gentle, dear and undefiled, (SC#8535). In other words, the image of Christ.

Upright means be straight or even, direct, fit and seem good, (SC#3474). This was the secret of Job's absolute commitment to God.

Proverbs 1:7 "The fear of the Lord is the beginning of knowledge." The result of the fear of the Lord in Job's life was humility. True humility represents Jesus.

Finally, Job hated and avoided evil. This characteristic made him an overcomer representing Jesus Christ who overcame the world.

Jesus, as Son of Man, was the second Adam. The depths to which Adam fell have only been superseded by the heights from which Christ came. Adam was created in the image, or resemblance, of God. In other words, he had an image. Let's consider some facts about Adam:

1. He was indecisive. He never chose the tree of life.
2. It was Adam's responsibility to instruct Eve. What instruction she received was confused.
3. Adam's dominion in the garden demanded he protect both his territory and Eve.
4. Adam saw another image, an angel of light, which he exchanged for the image of God. *Note: This image was religious as well as beguiling, crafty, unpredictable and treacherous.*
5. Adam justified his decision by blaming both Eve and God.
6. Adam's freedom of choice became independence from God.

Based on these considerations and knowing that Adam was created in the image of God, and that Jesus was the second Adam, or Man, we conclude that Adam was self-assured by nature. What about Jesus in His humanity? What was His nature? When asked to show the disciples the Father in John 14:8, 9, Jesus replied: *"he who has seen Me has seen the Father."* Truly, Christ saves us to the "uttermost." In all aspects that the first man with the image of God fell, the second Man with the image of God, is able to redeem.

There is a person coming soon on the world scene who will be beguiling, crafty, unpredictable and treacherous. He will require everyone to worship his **IMAGE**. This religious anti-Christ, or substitute Christ, will have an "angel of light" image and deceive multitudes. Beware of images!

Self-assured people, unless totally yielded to the Holy Spirit, have an unyielding spirit. This is because they are yielded to their image of self rather than yielded to God. The challenge to the self-assured believers in the Body of Christ is this: The one and only image which is acceptable for you is the image of Christ. What an awesome, challenging, powerful and beautiful reality! Your nature has been entrusted to you by God. Yours is the responsibility to present the true image of Christ to both the church and the world.

As the Holy Spirit began to unveil this information, Rayola was puzzled by the absence of a New Testament example of the self-assured person. She realized all of her examples of self-assured people who were overcomers came from the Old Testament. She asked the Lord to give her an overcoming New Testament self-assured person. The only New Testament person He would give her was shocking. The example was Jesus Christ, Himself.

Self-assured people, sacrifice your images, along with any lists against God, others or self, as well as pride, on the altar and allow the consuming fire of God to fall. In addition, the respect and acceptance you crave must be consistently given to others for whom Christ died so that Jesus, and Him alone, will be seen in your life.

The fourth gospel, the Gospel of John, testifies to Jesus as the Son of God. The submissive Apostle John penned this gospel by the Holy Ghost. The eagle represents the submissive nature. And the eagle is the king of all the birds.

Submissive people are unmanageable by nature and must become manageable under the wings of the Holy Spirit.

In the book of Revelation, the first words are *"The revelation of Jesus Christ."* Here we see John's perfect perspective. Remember, submissive people must press in for God's perspective. What greater perspective is there than Jesus Christ?

Job 39:27-29 reads: *"Does the eagle mount up at your command, and make her nest on high? She dwells and abides on the rock, upon the crag of the rock, and the strong place. From there she seeks the prey, and her eyes behold afar off,"* KJV. In these verses we realize that at God's command the eagle mounts up. This describes submissive people who know what they know in God and are eager to obey His commands. Like the eagle, submissive people who dwell and abide on the rock are secure on their "rock," Christ. And, from this heavenly perspective their eyes behold spiritual realms afar off.

The second thing we notice is that eagles mount higher and higher. Submissive people understand the ways of God when their analytical mind is under the control of God. How the Body of Christ needs to understand the ways of God!

Thirdly, Isaiah 40:31 says: *"But they that wait upon the Lord shall renew their strength; they shall mount up with wings as eagles; they shall run, and not be weary; and they shall walk, and not faint."* Submissive people who withdraw into God and wait for Him do mount up with strength. They are pillars in the church.

The fourth and final point, eagles are fearless. 2 Timothy 1:7: *"For God has not given us the spirit of fear; but of power, and of love, and of a sound mind."* Under the management of the Spirit of God, submissive people overcome their fears and are powerful in the kingdom of God.

Hebrews 12:3 tells us: *"For consider Him that endured such contradiction of sinners against Himself, least you be wearied and faint in your minds."* By replacing their own analytical ways with consideration of Christ, submissive believers can escape from weariness of mind which results in "fainting."

All conceit and fear must be sacrificed on the altar, and the acceptance submissive believers desire must be extended to others.

The submissive Apostle John said four things about himself in Revelation 1:9 which represents the overcoming submissive saint in the Body of Christ. They are: 1.) Your brother; 2.) Companion in tribulation; 3.) In the kingdom and 4.) In the patience of Jesus Christ. What valuable members of the church these often over-looked saints are! We are told in Galatians 2:9 that John was considered a "pillar" in the early church.

Submissive people's obedience to Christ will cause them to rise in faith to soar on the wind of the Holy Spirit. Remember, Jesus said that, *"we do not know where the wind comes from, nor can we know where it goes."* In other words, we cannot analyze it. But wings outstretched in faith and without fear, enable us to soar on the wind of the Holy Spirit, higher and higher, ever gaining God's perspective for the Body of Christ.

134

God is calling His church, people of all four natures, to be overcomers in these last days. If the strong-willed reflected the kingly attributes of Christ Jesus; if the stubborn are yoked with Christ as the living sacrifice; if the self-assured press through to attain the very image of Christ, and if the submissive gain the eagle's heavenly perspective of the ways of God, a dying world will be drawn to Christ! And finally, all the demons in hell won't be able to withstand the church of Jesus Christ!

(2 Samuel 22:36; 24:21 - 24; Zechariah 4:6; John 3:8; 16:33; Romans 5; 8:17; 1 Corinthians 15; 2 Corinthians 11:13-15; Galatians 5:16-23; Ephesians 5:21; 1 John 5:4 & 5; Revelation 12:9-11)

The Challenge to Come Higher

It is obvious God is not letting any of us off the hook. We must submit and become obedient under the mighty hand of God if we are going to overcome.

There is no other option for any of the natures, Jesus must be lifted up in each one to ensure that His character is worked within each believer. Therefore, the lion must become a lamb; the ox must be yoked to the only acceptable Sacrifice, Jesus; the man must take on the very image of Christ and the eagle must learn to soar on the wind of the Spirit.

The leadership potentials each nature can bring to the kingdom of God is awesome. The lion's decisive leadership actually prepares the way for the gospel to spread around the world just as the Apostle Paul did in Macedonia. The ox plows up the fallow hearts of men as Jeremiah did in his time. The man sows the seeds of the gospel as Christ; and the eagle oversees the work with the perspective of the Spirit as the Apostle John did in his writings.

In establishing the foundation of Christ in the church, the lion leads the way in laying the foundation. The ox follows in order to build the foundation. The man becomes the visible structure which serves as an example of the strength and validity of the foundation. The eagle protects both the foundation and structure from the heights of God. When it comes to the work of the cross in the lives of believers, we see the lion showing how to apply the cross. The ox prepares the way for the cross to be erected. The man is the visible product of the cross: the image of Christ coming forth in glory. The eagle signifies the victory of the cross: liberty in the Spirit to be all God intends us to be. In essence, our lives will become hid in Jesus and we will reflect the complete life of Christ. Jesus Christ is the *Hidden Manna*. But before He can be unveiled to the rest of the world, He must first be revealed to His followers. To partake of this Hidden Manna, we must mature in the knowledge of Jesus Christ.

Are you growing in Christ? Have you sat at the table to partake of the Hidden Manna? Is your life so hidden with Christ that you will be able to stand no matter what situation confronts you?

Part Four
Maturing in Christ

17

The Fragrance
of Christ

The church is to serve as a living sacrifice emitting the fragrance of Christ. This aroma draws the lost and enslaved to the Savior, and is a healing balm to those who are wounded, blind and deaf.

Each nature has their own abilities which play a different part in displaying the complete life of Christ to the world. The question is, how do each of these natures make up this fragrance?

In order to understand the fragrance of Christ, we must know Christ and be in relation ship with Him. One of the greatest revelations I received in my Christian walk was when the Lord told me I knew of Him and I knew about Him, but I did not know Him. What a surprise! After all, I had been a Christian for seven years.

Christ invited me to sit at His table to receive the hidden manna (partaking of His life). I realized I had settled for crumbs from other people. The Lord was now assuring me I could have a full meal.

The first time I came to His banquet table, I was afraid. I knew Scripture state Christ wants to be my friend, but no friendship had developed in those seven years. In time I did become comfortable as I started to enter into a friendship with Him. Eventually, I found myself serving this wonderful Friend.

Each time I obeyed my Lord's instruction, I moved closer to Him at His banquet table. In my training I became a committed student of the Holy Spirit, and this commitment meant listening for His voice and being obedient to the Word of God. I found that obedience is a learned response. This obedience involves a step by step response to whatever is before you. It comes out of sensitivity to God's heart and self-discipline.

The more sensitive and obedient I became to my Lord, the more intimate the relationship became. Love, peace and joy became by-products of this relationship.

During that time the Lord tore up a lot of turf in my life. He started with my perception of His identity and life. I had developed my own perception about Jesus, and this false perception put Christ in a small box and made me very self-righteous and judgmental to others. Of course, my perception never made me accountable. My fruit revealed someone who did not measure up, but my perception lied to me and told me I could contend with my own problems.

Eventually the real Jesus was able to break my perception. He took the Word of God and dissected me. He exposed my pride and broke me at the point of my strength. He gave me clarity about His nature, will and plan for my life.

Proverbs 4:7 instructs us to "...*get wisdom. Though it costs all you have, get understanding."* Jesus is the essence of our wisdom, but it is important that we understand His ways. To know Christ means to understand the way He does things. This understanding helps to develop the mind of Christ, which is contrary to human nature. The mind of Christ involves not only having the right attitude, but responding according to His ways.

(Matthew 7:20; 11:28-30; 22:1-14; 2 Corinthians 2:14 & 15; Galatians 5:22 & 23; Ephesians 5:2; Luke 16:10; John 6:32-35; 14:26; 15:9-14; Hebrews 3:9-14; 4:12)

Developing the Mind of Christ

Each person must challenge their perceptions and beliefs. Most subtle idolatry takes place in the mind. 2 Corinthians 10:5 instructs us to *"demolish arguments and every pretension that sets itself up against the knowledge of God and to take captive every thought to make it obedient to Christ."*

The preceptions differ with each nature, but are comprised of two major traits: pride and the strength each nature trusts in when making decisions. These beliefs determine what each nature considers to be "truth."

The problem with this so-called "truth" based on the nature's reference is that it will reject the real Truth. The Truth is the Jesus of the Bible. The pride of each nature will ultimately create a false perception of Jesus, and in subtle ways will exalt itself against the knowledge of God. This subtle exultation will keep God from being God in our lives. For this reason pride must be mortified or be put to death on a daily basis.

Obedience to Christ comes out of faith but each nature has a tendency to put faith in its own strengths. As stated previously, these strengths must be disciplined. They actually give us a delusion about our own ability to make things right. These strengths in fact, give us a false sense of elitism which cleverly entitles us to judge those who do not agree with us.

Consider each nature's frame of reference:

Nature	Pride Mortify	Strength Discipline
Submissive	Conceit (Pride)	Analytical Mind
Stubborn	Standard (Pride)	Emotions
Self-Assured	Image (Pride)	Standards
Strong-Willed	Control (Pride)	Conclusions (Right/Wrong)

Wrong beliefs result in a wrong spirit behind all actions. A wrong spirit indicates that a person's reactions are based on their perception of self, instead of reactions which are based on who Jesus Christ is. Therefore, it is not surprising to see King David pray that God will not only *create a clean heart, but renew a right spirit within him.*

When pride reigns it actually feeds our strengths with a false sense of power which may drive people to extremes. For example, the submissive person's intellectual conclusions will become unmanageable. If the conclusions are not challenged, the individual may end up out of touch with reality. The stubborn person will prove to be very undisciplined in their emotions. These emotions can make them seem as unstable as high waves on the ocean and make them appear unrealistic. The self-assured person creates unobtainable standards to maintain their images. These standards can make them appear foolish and unyielding to realistic godly standards and attitudes. The strong-willed person will believe they are right and will become unruly when challenged to reconsider this position. They will maintain their belief to their own destruction.

The only correct frames of reference on which the natures are to be grounded are spirit and truth. The spirit of course, is the Spirit of God. The Holy Spirit is the only One who leads us into all truth about Jesus. Jesus is our only example. He came from the majesty of heaven to take on the nature of a man and a servant. He was obedient to the Father. His obedience required Him to humble Himself. This humility resulted in His submission to the cross. His responses show each of us what it means to have the mind of Christ.

Pride is contrary to the mind of Christ. It does not hold people personally accountable for ungodly attitudes and actions. It sacrifices others and refuses to submit. It encourages the elitism which makes an individual judge of all matters.

Truth makes an individual free. The Holy Spirit brings liberty. It is only within the boundaries of the Spirit and Truth that we can worship our God.

True worship requires sacrifice. Self must be sacrificed in order to worship God. Worship means we have entered the Holy of Holies to minister to our God. It is in the Holy of Holies that an intimate relationship is established. This intimacy allows the life of Jesus, *the living manna,* to be imparted to us so we are brought to perfection in Him.

Let's now consider how each nature represents the mind of Christ. The mind of Christ means the Holy Spirit is reigning in truth. Compare the description of the mind of Christ found in Philippians 2:5-8:

Nature	Right Spirit	Truth Attitude
Submissive	Manageable	Submission
Stubborn	Disciplined	Obedient
Self-Assured	Yielded	Humbled
Strong-Willed	Ruled	Cross (Death)

Are you representing the mind of Christ to a dying world?

(Philippians 2:5-11; Romans 12:1; John 4:23 & 24; 8:31-36; 14:6 16:13-15; 1 Peter 1; 2 Peter 1:3-11)

The Heart of Christ

There are two words which describe the heart of Christ: *unconditional love.* John 3:16 says it well, *"For God so loved the world that he gave his one and only Son, that whoever believes in him shall not perish but have eternal life."* Matthew 6:21 goes one step further with this statement, *"For where your treasure is, there your heart will be also."*

We gain an insight into God's heart in these two scriptures. First of all, His heart is where his treasure is and His treasure happens to be people. We therefore, must become involved with people if we want to know God's heart. This involvement implies becoming vulnerable to people.

John 2:24 & 25 tells us that, *"Jesus did not commit Himself to man; for he knew what was in them."* It is important to understand Jesus did not submit to man's whims, but He did submit to God's will and plan for man. God's will for man brought Christ to the cross where He became vulnerable to man's rejection, persecution, torture and death.

Jesus told His followers to be, *"as wise as serpents and as harmless as doves."* To be vulnerable requires wisdom as to the manner in which we serve people.

Godly wisdom is pure, peace-loving, considerate, submissive, merciful, impartial and sincere. To act wisely, our motives must be pure. The only acceptable motive is a need to see and know God with the desire to do what is pleasing and acceptable to Him. In order to see God we must have a child-like relationship with Him. Remember, we can only lead someone to where we are with God.

A right relationship will produce the responses of peace and love. Peace will be evident because we are at peace with our God. Love will come forth because our God, who is the essence of love, resides in our hearts. Godly love is a commitment to be right before God and do right by others.

John instructs us to *"not just love in words, but in deeds."* He also poses this provoking thought, *"If anyone says, 'I love God,' yet hates his brother, he is a liar. For anyone who does not love his brother, whom he has seen, cannot love God, whom he has not seen. And he has given us this command: whoever loves God must also love his brother."* John is telling us that we can gauge how we are responding to God by how we treat those around us.

God's love will never sacrifice others. It will never strip people of their dignity. It will show respect and be considerate of the plight of individuals.

The next step of godly wisdom is to identify a Christian's position in the kingdom of God. The position is that of a committed servant. A servant is in tune with their Lord's goals. They belong to him and have no personal rights.

Lordship, for the Christian, implies self has lost much of its power and reign in a person's life. Self is being replaced with the mercy of God. Mercy is at the heart of servitude in the kingdom of God.

It is from a heart of mercy, that an abundant life is produced. This abundant life is the result of abiding in the One who shows mercy to each of us on a daily basis. His name is Jesus.

Jesus is the vine. He gives us life. This life displays the fruit of the Spirit which attracts others to the Vine.

This wisdom is not partial. It does not consider service in light of personal gain and recognition. We are co-laborers with Christ. He alone deserves the glory for whatever is accomplished in the spiritual realm. He came to save the most unlovable people including wretched individuals such as me.

God's wisdom is sincere. There is nothing fake about its motives, commitments or responses. It inspires a relationship with God and makes the Word of God come alive. Everything that is done, is done for the glory of the Living God.

Godly wisdom does give us healthy boundaries. It serves as a wall of protection against ignorance and naivete. It keeps Satan from accusing an individual when their motives are correct. It exposes self, giving an individual the power to overcome. It maintains a godly perspective - keeping a person from touching God's glory in their service to others. It desires the will of God over personal preferences. Right now test your life before God and see what it may be telling you about your heart condition.

Proverbs 4:23 tells us to *"guard your heart, for it is the wellspring of life."* Our reactions will tell us whether Christ is reigning.

We have already made reference to the type of heart each nature can display. We know the submissive person has a sweet, sensitive heart. Jesus said of the pondering Nathaniel, there was no guile in him. Here we see someone with a sincere, open heart. The minute Nathaniel encountered the real Jesus, he recognized and acknowledged Him. A sincere heart desires the real thing and approaches God with the determination and a child-like acceptance of a Daniel.

The stubborn King David had a perfect heart. He trusted in his God and was honest about his life before his Creator and Judge. David's psalms show us he had peace with his God and an unwavering love for Him. His relationship with God determined his responses towards others. He was long-suffering with King Saul, committed to Jonathan, wise in the handling of his enemies and open to Abigail's intercession for her household and open to Nathan's reproof of his sin.

The self-assured person must have a servant's heart. For the self-assured individual to have this heart they must see God. After Moses' various encounters with God, he showed consideration for Israel when he selflessly offered himself on their behalf. In the cases of Moses and Jacob we see two men submitting to God for purpose and direction. For both Jacob and Job, we see two men, broken and humbled before God, ready to please Him.

In the case of the Apostle Paul, we see a harsh persecutor of Christians. After Christ redirected Paul, he developed a singleness of heart in obedience to His new Lord. He showed unlimited mercy and compassion to the lost Gentiles. He became impartial to religion, race and culture; a sincere crusader for the liberty of enslaved and hurting souls. What a picture of a changed heart.

Insight of the acceptable heart conditions of each nature gives us a picture of Christ's heart. Let us now examine the heart of Christ.

Nature	Christ's Heart
Submissive	Sincere (Motive-Attitude)
Stubborn	Perfect (Maturity-Righteous)
Self-Assured	Servant (Position-Relationship)
Strong-Willed	Singleness (Obedient-Response)

Does your heart reflect the heart of Christ?

(1 Samuel 18:1-4; 19; 23:1-23; 24; 25; 26; 2 Samuel 1; 9; 12; 1 Kings 2:1-9; 3:14; 8:23-26, 60 & 61; Matthew 5:9; 10:16; John 1:45-51; 1 Corinthians 1:29-31; Ephesians 2:13-18; James 3:17; 1 John 3:14-18; 4:8-21)

Christ the Rock

Now we must consider the relationship each nature must have with Christ. This relationship will be determined by our response to Jesus as our spiritual foundation.

Submissive people must know Jesus as the foundation or rock in which they place their confidence. The more they learn to put their faith in Christ, the more steady they become as a pillar in the church. When submissive people resort to hiding in the cleft of the Rock during the storms of life, the greater their perspective becomes. The more they withdraw and wait upon their Rock, the faster they will relinquish all of their fears and rights. This will allow them the freedom to spread out their wings in confidence and soar on the wind of the Holy Spirit.

Stubborn natured people must align their spiritual life to their Cornerstone, Jesus. According to a builder, all other stones are lined up to the cornerstone. Stubborn people must therefore, adjust their lives to the Word of God. This alignment will make stubborn individuals stable in their trust in Christ. As they realize that their Cornerstone is immovable and trustworthy, they will become bold in their faith in their Lord. This boldness will make them powerful in their prayer closet and in their battle against Satan.

Self-assured people must gain both assurance of and insight into who Jesus really is in power and authority. Jacob encountered Jesus in the form of a Stone on which he laid his head, and acquired an assurance about God's interest and plan for his life. Moses gained insight into Jesus as the Rock in the wilderness when Christ miraculously supplied living water to the thirsty Nation of Israel.

To self-assured people Jesus is symbolic as the Rock. Keep in mind, a self-assured person is to be the representation of Christ, the man, to our lost world. However, this representation does not occur if they handle the things of God incorrectly. Moses abused the rock, keeping him out of the promised land. Jacob on the other hand, took his rock (stone) erected and anointed it. Self-assured people must realize that the Holy Spirit, the Living Water, anoints them with power and authority as the life of Jesus is erected in their life. It is Jesus' presence in and around them that gives them assurance and power. For a self-assured person to take credit for the things of God is to abuse the very life and power of Christ in their lives.

Jesus refers to Himself as a Rock of judgment which either breaks an individual or falls on them. Judgment implies separation. We see Christ serving as a Rock of judgment to the strong-willed person. This rock was prevalent in the life of King Nebuchadnezzar.

King Nebuchadnezzar had a dream about a great image. This image represented the world being ruled by four kingdoms. In his dream a stone smote the image and broke it into many pieces. The stone was Christ who one day would break the power of all nations and take His rightful place as Ruler.

Strong-willed people must be broken at the point of their control. This control subtly makes them rulers in their established domain. Christ will become a decisive Rock of judgment which will bring a separation in their life. Either they will come under Jesus' rule or they will find the Stone destroying their control and domain.

Paul was broken on the road to Damascus. He chose to come under the leadership of Christ. As a result he was used as a special vessel to carry the message of the cross to the world. The message was a stumbling block to the Jews and foolishness to the Gentiles.

The cross represents judgment. It brings separation in our lives as follows:

Satan	vs.	Christ
Self	vs.	Holy Spirit
Sin	vs.	God's Grace
Religion	vs.	Relationship
	(Equals)	
Bondage	vs.	Liberty
(Death)		(Life)

The Apostle Paul was totally pre-occupied with preaching the message of the cross. He presented the choices of the cross, which caused a separation in the hearts and lives of people.

Paul had learned to follow the real Jesus. His leadership brought decisive judgment to the new churches. He challenged Christians with godly instruction and counsel. He called them to accountability in relationships, attitudes and conduct. He brought clarity to issues confronting the different bodies of believers. Today his judgments continue to serve as guidelines for believers.

The Apostle Paul not only expounded about the cross of Christ, but about his own cross. Paul knew the power and authority that came from the application of both crosses to his life. As he applied his cross to his self-rule, Christ was lifted up in his life. As Christ was lifted up in Paul's life, the power was there to draw men to the salvation Christ obtained for man on His cross.

Paul not only preached the cross, he lived according to the cross. He not only instructed people about their cross, he was an example of how the cross is applied to self. He was a leader who knew his place, responsibility and authority.

Paul knew his life was hid in Christ and that anything outside of Christ was "dung". He said this about his responsibility, *"For I resolved to know nothing while I was with you except Jesus Christ and him crucified."* He added this insight about the source of his power and authority from in Philippians 3:10 & 11 and 2 Timothy 2:11 & 12, *"I want to know Christ and the power of his resurrection and the fellowship of sharing in his sufferings, becoming like him in his death, and so, somehow, to attain to the resurrection from the dead... If we died with him, we will also live with him; if we (suffer), we will also reign with him."*

The Apostle Paul knew in whom he believed, and had total trust in Him. He had suffered much to know Christ's power and in the end he died for His precious Lord. Since Paul had become identified with Christ, he could with great expectation pen this victorious statement just before his death, *"I have fought the good fight, I have finished the race, I have kept the faith. Now there is in store for me the crown of righteousness, which the Lord, the righteous Judge, will award to me on that day--and not only to me, but also to all who have longed for his appearing."*

As you can see each nature has a different relationship with Christ, their Rock. These different relationships determine how the natures represent Christ to the world. Together the natures present a complete picture of Christ's work among His followers. Let us now examine the picture:

Nature	Christ-Rock	Representation	Results
Submissive	Rock	Pillar	Confidence
Stubborn	Cornerstone	Stone	Boldness
Self-Assured	Symbol Image	Anointing	Assurance
Strong-Willed	Judgment	Power	Authority

(Genesis 28:10-22, 35:9-15; Numbers 20:7-13 refer to 1 Corinthians 10:4; Song of Solomon 2:14; Isaiah 40:31; Daniel 2:44 & 45; Matthew 15:1-9; 16:17-19; 23; Luke 20:17 & 18; Romans 5:19-21; 8:14-17; 1 Corinthians 2:2-5; 15:31; Galatians 2:20; 4:19-5:1, 17-25; 6:14; Philippians 3:7-9; 2 Timothy 1:12; 4:7 & 8; Hebrews 4:12-16; 1 Peter 2:5-8)

The Essence of Christ

The church is the essence of Christ's life. This spiritual entity represents the mind, heart, position and authority of Christ to the dying world. We can actually see each nature serving as a distinct depiction of Christ in these different areas. This picture comes into focus when you consider the strengths of each nature. These strengths of course, must be under the power of the Holy Spirit. Let me show you how these strengths symbolize Christ:

150

Nature	Right Spirit	Strength	Christ
Submissive	Manageable	Analytical Mind	Mind
Stubborn	Disciplined	Emotions-Love	Heart
Self-Assured	Yielded	Image-Servant	Position
Strong-Willed	Ruled	Lines-Judgment	Authority

Each of these strengths determine how God reveals Himself to each nature. For example, the Holy Spirit shows Himself to the submissive nature through their analytical mind. The mind of the submissive individual needs details in order to draw wise conclusions about situations. The Holy Spirit reveals God by teaching the submissive person the ways of God. These ways give an orderly description of how God works consistently in the lives of people. The submissive person who knows the ways of God gains confidence in Him because He is consistent and can be understood. Understanding God's ways enables the submissive person to bring God's perspective to the church through challenging instruction and with a child-like example.

The Holy Spirit reveals God to the stubborn person through their emotions. Stubborn people experience God in His creation, art and music. The Holy Spirit uses these expressions to demonstrate God's reality to the world.

The stubborn individual can be very loving and compassionate, but also can serve as a stubborn plumb-line in the things of God. They can express their love for God through ministry in the arts, or they can display a righteous indignation for unholy alliances in people's lives. They can show great tolerance for others or be blunt and judgmental. They appear to be a paradox, and yet to God they are powerful leaders and soldiers in the kingdom of God. In fact, they can serve as a prophetic voice to the church.

The Holy Spirit reveals Christ to the self-assured through images. For this to happen, all wrong concepts must be destroyed. Christ not only took on the form of a man, but he became a servant. The image that must be exalted is that of a servant. Servitude is contrary to pride which motivates bad attitudes. It is submissive in attitude, humble in spirit and obedient in response. It only pays homage to the true Lord. It honors others above self and desires to exalt the Lord of lords. It ultimately sacrifices for the benefit of others and the glory of God. Therefore, the attitude, spirit (heart) and response of the self-assured person, who has been conformed to the image of Christ, serves as a true image and example of Jesus Christ to the church and the world.

The Holy Spirit discloses Christ to the strong-willed nature through factual encounters and decisive experiences. Christ gives them the facts by showing Himself to them, then He channels them by using extreme experiences. These experiences offer them choices. The choice is death to self-rule in order to gain spiritual life, or self-rule which will end in spiritual death. In my studies I noticed that there was a smaller circle of men found among the disciples. Jesus, of course called three men apart just as He does each believer. They were Peter, John and James. We know thesubmissive

John represented the eagle, Peter, the stubborn ox, Jesus the man, but what about James? If these four were to depict the total image of Christ to the world, James had to be the strong-willed lion. We know that he followed Jesus immediately after he was called, and he wanted to call fire from heaven on the Samaritans. This could imply he was being decisive in his decisions to follow Jesus and to address the Samaritan's response to Jesus. The only other detail we have about James is that he was the first martyr of the apostles. He was killed by Herod's sword in Acts 12:2.

We know that the strong-willed person must put to death self-rule. We see James becoming a martyr in the early stages of the church. The next strong-willed person we can clearly observe in Scripture is the Apostle Paul. Paul was called to be a martyr as well. He suffered and then died for the sake of Christ. Here we see the complete work of the cross in the lives of both men: death and suffering. Remember, the lion shows the way to the cross. What is the real purpose of the cross? It can be found in the meaning of the word "martyr" which means witness.

Christians are called to be witnesses of Christ and His salvation. They are given the authority and power to be effective witnessess. This life-changing testimony will not have authority and power until death and suffering occur.

Christ had to die to establish a new testament or covenant between man and God. Christ not only established a new testament, but His death gave it power and authority to be activated in the lives of people.

We see the gospel being made real by the sacrificial life of Paul. He was a living martyr (witness) of the salvation of God. He experienced daily death in order to have authority and he suffered to obtain resurrected power. Authority and power only come by way of the cross. Judgments or conclusions can only be righteous when aligned with the cross which displays the unconditional love of Christ and the judgment for sin.

153

The cross is God's mercy coming together with His righteousness. It is the light of God exposing the darkness; His love overcoming hatred and punishment; the only avenue of hope which inspires faith and subdues fear. A strong-willed individual can bring clarity of the cross, separation to the church and serve as a powerful witness to the world.

For the church to demonstrate the essence of Christ, there must be total submission of mind, heart and position to the cross as a sacrifice. The cross brings a brokenness. This brokenness allows Christ to be lifted up. As the church becomes a living sacrifice, Christ will be raised up in spirit and truth in His body. His presence will serve as a sweet fragrance to God and will draw the world to His salvation.

(Luke 9:51-56; John 12:32; Romans 12:1; 1 Corinthians 15:31; Hebrews 9:11-28)

18

Ministering the Life of Christ

Christians have a commission to preach the Gospel and to make disciples for Christ. This commission is not optional, but a responsibility of all who claim Christ. In fact, Christians are to be ambassadors...official representatives of the kingdom of heaven.

I realize there are some Christians who simply want to benefit from the hope of Christ without paying a price. They may even believe they are rich like those of the church at Laodicea in Revelation 3:14-20. But the truth is, they lack love for their God.

The solution to most of what ails us as Christians can be solved by falling in love with the Jesus of the Bible. It is lack of God's love which produces a wrong spirit in our lives. It is God's love which inspires us to adhere to our commission in spirit and truth. Let me share with you in a simple way to understand what constitutes a right spirit or a wrong spirit.

A person's motivation, intention and goals are influenced by their spirit. The results or fruit produced in that person's life indicates whether their spirit is right or wrong. Compare the differences between a right and wrong spirit.

	Right Spirit	Wrong Spirit
Motivation:	The love of God	Pride
Intention:	To glorify God	To exalt self
Goal (Truth):	To lift up JESUS	To lift up self
Results:	Liberty-Potential Fruit of the Spirit	Control-Bondage Strife & Contention

Jesus said of the religious Pharisees in Matthew 15:8 & 9, *"These people honor me with their lips, but their hearts are far from me. They worship in vain; their teachings are but rules taught by men."* The religious people of Jesus' day could talk the talk but they were hypocrites.

As we can see, the right spirit will enable a person to effectively worship and serve God to the fullest. The wrong spirit will exalt man, making him a little god. This requires man to control everything around him. Control creates bondage and oppression for anyone who may be within its range.

The quality of man's spirit dictates where his faith will rest. The right spirit puts faith in the one true God, but the wrong spirit puts trust in self. We read this instruction from Paul in 2 Corinthians 13:5, *"Examine yourselves to see whether you are in the faith; test yourselves. Do you not realize that Christ Jesus is in you--unless of course, you fail the test."*

We must love God to insure a right spirit. The right spirit is under the control of the Holy Spirit who leads an individual into all truth. Jesus is truth, therefore the right spirit will lead you to the revelation of Truth Personified.

Jesus gave this commandment in Mark 12:30, *"Love the Lord your God with all your heart and with all your soul and with all your mind and with all your strength,..."* Here we see four areas which typify a complete love for God. These four responses of love correlates with the four natures. For example:

Submissive--Love God with all your mind.
(Understanding)
Stubborn--Love God with all your heart.
(Emotions)
Self-Assured--Love God with all your soul.
(Will, Emotions, Mind-Self)
Strong-Willed--Love God with all your strength.
(Everything you have in you.)

We must have a love relationship with our Lord in order to be effective. To have such a relationship requires us to sit at the table with Jesus and learn of Him. The table offers a feast. The Living Water of the Holy Spirit is abundantly available. The Hidden Manna will be imparted to you.

It is at the table where we will be clothed in Christ's righteousness, and find His will for our lives, our position in His body and our place of service in the world. It is at His table we begin to learn true obedience.

Once we get to know our Lord, we will know what pleases Him. His heart is with people. Therefore true ministry is not only standing behind a pulpit, but standing in the trenches with hurting people as well. It is not being obvious in service to others that makes one great, but being willing to serve in obscurity and faithfulness where only God can see you.

The key to ministry is knowing Jesus. How can I preach with authority if I do not know Christ? How can I pour the life of Christ into others, if His life is not being worked into me? How can I make people students of Christ when I have never learned to be His devoted follower? How can I get people into the Holy of Holies when I have not been there? If I know Christ in a personal way, He will be lifted up and he will validate my life and testimony.

I know in my case God had to redefine ministry. As I began to realize that effective ministry may be sending a card to a lonely or sick person, cleaning a toilet, taking food to the sick or calling someone to encourage them, I began to understand how opportunities to minister may be missed. Pleasing ministry is so practical, anyone can do it.

Recently, I found my idea of ministry being challenged. A certain individual implied that if I was not willing to compromise in the area of ministry, I would never get into churches to share what God has given me. I pondered this threat. I concluded that as long as this ministry remained in God's hands, He would open doors of opportunity. I also realized ministry was all around me simply because I would never run out of hurting and lost souls.

Christians need to redefine ministry. Ministry is practical and the opportunities to minister daily are numerous. The key is availability and sensitivity to the Holy Spirit. We are servants and soldiers who have no personal rights outside of what our Lord and Commander has established in the Word of God. We must ensure liberty in the Spirit, not only for ourselves, but others in order to reach our potential. We must avoid gossip, pat answers, personal causes, and touching God's glory and work with our miserable flesh and pride. We must listen with our hearts and be humble in attitude.

These qualities are necessary if we are going to minister the life of Jesus to others. Remember, it is Christ who sets the captive free, heals the broken hearted, gives sight to the blind and hearing to the deaf. We can do nothing apart from Him.

What we can do is understand how to minister to the individual natures. By understanding how to address their need based on their nature, we can breech their walls of mistrust. Here are some simple keys to opening up the different natures in order to minister to them.

Submissive people need acceptance. Keep in mind they do have a sweet heart and many fears. By acknowledging their sweet heart and their fear of failure you are communicating acceptance to them. This will open them up to allow you to speak into their life.

Stubborn individuals need you to enter in with them emotionally. Because they are emotionally sensitive, most likely they have been hurt, misunderstood and feel guilty and insecure. By recognizing their emotional plight, you will beentering in with them. This will serve as proof that you care about them.

Self-assured people have high standards due to their image. In approaching them show the same type of respect to them you would Moses. Acknowledge you recognize they have set tough standards for themselves, and may feel frustrated and angry if the standards haven't been met. Encourage them to give themselves a break. Once they give themselves a break, they will be able to give others a break.

Strong-willed individuals are diamonds. This means they probably have found themselves in extreme situations. By recognizing they are a diamond you can open them up. For example I have said to some strong-willed people, "You remind me of a valuable diamond. I bet you have been through some difficulties in your life." If this is so, they will agree and share with you what they have encountered.

This gives you an idea how to reach each nature, but keep in mind that the Holy Spirit is the real Counselor. He is able to give you insight and the key into people's lives. Learn to rely on Him and you will acquire the wisdom to scripturally counsel and minister to people.

19

Identifying Satan's Tactics for Each Nature

Today there is much confusion concerning what constitutes rebellion or demonic influences in a person. For instance, some think"Satan is behind every evil act of man" while others believe that "demonic influences" happen in Africa, but not in America." People either glorify Satan or ignore his tactics altogether. Both extremes delight Satan.

There is a difference between rebellion and demonic influence, oppression and possession.

Rebellion means the person is operating in a wrong spirit. This opens the door for Satan to oppress their souls, which is nothing more than bondage. James 4:7 instructs rebellious Christians to, "*Submit yourselves, then, to God. Resist the devil, and he will flee from you.*"(KJV) Repentance of rebellion closes the door to any spiritual oppression. Once the door is closed, Satan must flee.

Possession is the result of unchecked oppression which turns into obsession. Obsession is demonic control of a person's soul and spirit as was the case with King Saul. It does not mean this demonic influence is constant.

The question is, how do I tell the difference between rebellion and demonic influence. Rebellion will fluctuate while demonic influence is an unmovable wall. People who are under the influence of demonic spirits appear to be unable to hear or see, or understand what you are saying. It is as if you hit a wall.

Rebellion must be correctly challenged, while demonic influence must be put down with the authority of Christ. (I am not talking about deliverance.) The goal in putting down the forces of darkness is to give the person a choice between liberty in Christ or bondage and control under Satan.

In the following pages, Jeannette gives us insight about what weaknesses Satan will use in each nature to bring them into bondage and under his control. You will see there are two major doors which give Satan access to our lives. They include: pride and fear. The final product is delusion.

******

There are three things the Word of God tells us we must overcome; namely, the world, the flesh and the devil. The world consists of doing that which is necessary. The necessities of life are neither good nor evil, but Jesus warns us that these daily cares, along with the deceitfulness of riches, can choke out the Word of God in our lives causing us to become unfruitful. Christians need to be keenly aware of which "necessities" of life are actually replacing the Word of God on a daily basis.

The flesh represents doing that which is natural. Because of our fallen nature and distorted perceptions, Christians must allow the Word of God to challenge what seems normal or right to them. Romans 8:13 & 14 tells us, *"For if you live after the flesh, you shall die; but if you through the spirit do mortify (put to death) the deeds of the body, you shall live. For as many as are led by the Spirit of God, they are the sons of God."*(KJV) As you understand the traits of your own nature and examine them in light of God's Word, you will gain insight as to what needs to be mortified and what needs to be brought under the control of the Spirit.

The devil causes activity which is not natural. In other words, unnatural thoughts and actions. Unnatural means "not normal; artificial or affected; cruel or inhuman." When demonic influence is active in a person's life, attitudes and behavior results which are contrary to that person's actual nature.

The Submissive Nature

The natural tnedency of this nature is to be unmanageable. If this nature does not allow the Holy Spirit to continually manage them, then Satan takes advantage of this form of independence. Furthermore, because this nature has to continually deal with fear, Satan can amplify this problem by bringing a spirit of fear against them. Remember 2 Timothy 1:7 promises, *"For God has not given us the spirit of fear; but of power, and love, and of a sound mind."*(KJV)

There is a natural, God-given fear-- the kind of fear which helps preserve our lives by instinctively keeping us from foolish actions such as playing in the middle of the freeway! However, unnatural fear and demonic influence can cause the submissive person to lose faith and cave in to a type of spiritual paralysis. Fear can be one of the greatest means of defeat for this nature.

Conceit, a form of pride, is also an open door for the enemy. When a submissive person puts their confidence in their own intellectual prowess rather than in God, they have just committed idolatry. Proverbs 26:12 tells us, *"Do you see a man wise in his own conceit? There is more hope for a fool than him."* (KJV) This is because he is now depending on himself to be his own savior.

The tendency to over-analyze is the third area this nature needs to overcome. Philippians 2:3-5 tells us to *have the mind of Christ*. But fear of failure, conceit and dependence on their own analytical ways, may open the door to Satanic deception.

Finally, when a submissive person becomes out-of-balance in the extreme actual demonic possession can take place. This nature needs to beware of excessive dramatization which can result in horrible actions.

Submissive people can easily exchange proper Biblical meditation for "mystical meditations" resulting in a type of pseudo spirituality which is actually occultic spiritualism. Delusion at this stage can be full blown including a religious spirit, or a familiar spirit, complete with acceptable "Christian terminology."

Remember, this nature does not have an "image" of self. When a submissive person consistently exhibits an "image", this "image" is nothing less than demonic.

The submissive nature needs to continually ask God for His perspective, they also need to overcome the tendency to rely on their own analytical mind.

Finally, remember the submissive Apostle John, who asked permission to call fire out of heaven and was rebuked by Christ who told him he knew not what spirit he was of.

The Stubborn Nature

People who are stubborn by nature have a tremendous capacity for deep emotions. And because their perception is based on their emotions, Satanic influence can persuade, manipulate and delude them emotionally. Also, lying spirits routinely torment people of this nature. These spirits can enter into the stubborn person's flights of fantasy, daydreams, night dreams, insecurities and fears. The result can be tremendous guilt and loss of faith.

Satan also takes advantage of the stubborn person's need for "proof," and he often offers such "proof" in the form of delusions of past lives (reincarnation) and other powers, like telepathy. He is also able to push this nature's emotional buttons to commit crimes of passion.

Fear, caused by emotional guilt, depression and a feeling of hopelessness, along with doubt of God's love and forgiveness, enables the enemy to undermine this nature's faith and push them into wrong decisions. Stubborn people need to keep Proverbs 3:5, 6 in mind, (*"Trust in the Lord with all your heart; and lean not unto your own understanding. In all your ways acknowledge him, and he shall direct your paths."*) (KJV)

Stubbornness itself is an entrance to demonic oppression and possible possession, as 1 Samuel 15:22, 23 warns us, *"For rebellion is as the sin of witchcraft, and stubbornness is as iniquity and idolatry."*(KJV) Remember, it is idolatry to exalt anything or anyone above God including faith in that stubborn wall, rather than in God's ability to judge righteously in our lives.

This nature also needs to be alert to any root of bitterness, unforgiveness or judgmentalism because Satan gains entrance through these attitudes.

Finally, remember even Peter was rebuked by Christ when He said, *"Get thee behind me Satan: for you are an offense to me: for you do not savour the things that be of God, but those that be of men."* (KJV)

God is calling this nature to overcome by becoming yoked with Jesus Christ. By being yoked with Christ, the stubborn nature will become disciplined through learning and applying God's Word.

The Self-Assured Nature

Because the self-assured nature has an unyielding spirit in the natural, it is easy for Satan to bring delusion. This is accomplished through the pride they have in their own image of self. Proverbs 11:2 reads, *"When pride comes, then comes shame: but with the lowly is wisdom."* (KJV)

Self-assured people must be aware of the danger of yielding to their own image rather than to Jesus Christ. Satan's downfall came because of pride and so it is with mankind. Pride always goes before a fall!

Fear is another entrance for the enemy, and in the case of self-assured people, remember their greatest fear is incompetence. Proverbs 29:25 says, *"The fear of man brings a snare: but whoso puts his trust in the Lord shall be safe."* (KJV)

Because of their image, delusion can overtake their reasoning ability. Naturally, when this occurs Satan masterfully manipulates both their emotions and perceptions until they actually believe a lie. This "lie" can be perceived as truth by the self-assured person and it can include both their own perception of self and others. When this nature is operating under any kind of delusion, two extremes occur-- the first elevates their image of self and the other casts suspicion, and falsely accuses others.

Of course, much of the delusion and double-mindedness this nature may experience is also based on their "list." As explained earlier in this book, this list justifies un-Christlike actions. And with demonic assistance, these actions can be extremely violent, unmerciful and unthinkable to the natural mind.

Proverbs 14:12 gravely warns, *"There is a way which seems right unto a man, but the end thereof are the ways of death."*(KJV) And Matthew 5:22 records these words of Jesus, *"But I say to you, that whosoever is angry with his brother without a cause shall be in danger of the judgment."*(KJV)

It is sad but true that most violent crimes are committed by people of this nature. The self-assured believer must overcome by yielding to Christ's image through absolute faith in Him rather than his own images. Otherwise, Satan will erect an image for his own purposes which will ultimately have the power to delude and destroy others who "believe" in it, including the self-assured person .

The Strong-Willed Nature

The vulnerability to demonic influence in this nature occurs because of unruliness, control, pride and a sense of infallibility.

This nature can actually believe Satan never lies to them and that every thought they have is of God! Couple this concept with pride and a determination to control others and you have witchcraft.

Strong-willed people must believe God when He tells us in Proverbs 16:18, *"Pride goes before destruction, and an haughty spirit before a fall."*(KJV) An insistence on maintaining pride, control and drawing their own concuclusions will ultimately end in defeat for these people.

This dynamic nature does well to have wise and godly advisors. Proverbs 12:15 reminds us, *"The way of a fool is right in his own eyes: but he that hearkens to counsel is wise."*(KJV) Satan loves to delude these factual people into thinking that their beliefs are always God's will when just the opposite is true.

People with this nature need to humble themselves, come under the rule of the Holy Spirit and have faith in God alone!

Hidden Manna

****

It is obvious the goal of Satan is to delude man. Consider what each nature must beware of to avoid Satan's delusion:

Natures:	Submissive	Stubborn	Self Assured	Strong Willed
Beware:	Fear Conceit Mind	Emotions Fear Stubborn	Image Fear Anger	Conclusions Pride Control
Delusion:	Image Control	Judgmental Unmerciful	Hatred Murder	Infallible Fear of losing control Witchcraft

(1 Samuel 15:22 & 23;18:5-16; Matthew 13:22; 16:23; Luke 9:55)

20

Becoming
Precious Gemstones

God is a God of order. He expresses the different facets of His nature through three persons, God the Father, God the Son and God the Holy Spirit. Why would He not express Himself differently through four natures? These natures relate to God in distinct ways, and perceive Him according to their own frame of reference. This explains why God would use these qualities to reveal Himself to each nature.

God never works outside of His nature, nor is His relationship with his people contrary to their nature. That is why God works with and uses these natures differently. In combination, the natures represent the Universal Christ whose power and authority extends to all corners of the world through the Holy Spirit working in and through His church.

To represent Christ in this fashion, these natures must be brought to perfection. This perfection involves a process.

The process behind our spiritual perfection, relates to the four cups at Passover. These cups represent the four expressions found in Exodus 6:6 & 7:

I will Free you
I will Deliver you
I will Redeem you
I will Take you (to be My People)

The first cup has to do with sanctification. This involves preparation to receive what God has for us. This work is done by the Word of God and the Holy Spirit. The Word has a lot to do with our faith. It serves as a hammer to destroy wrong concepts, and a sword which exposes our spiritual ineptness. We either let God be God because our perception is scriptural or we limit Him, and never come to full knowledge of Him.

The Holy Spirit sets our priorities and relationships in order. He transforms our minds and lives making us into new creations. To accomplish such a feat He must have liberty. There are three enemies that threaten this liberty. They are: sin, self and religion. These three ingredients can:

Cage the lion
Muzzle the ox
Enslave the man
Bind the eagle

Power and authority will only come when there is liberty to reach our potential. By stifling any of these natures, the church will suffer in these areas:

170

Eagle-Lack Heavenly Perspective
Ox-Silence the Prophetical Voice
Man-Miss the Example of the Real Jesus
Lion-Limit the Work and Authority of the Cross

The second cup has to do with <u>deliverance</u> from judgment. God often uses Satan in this area. Satan brings the separation which creates a refinement in the person. God then, delivers the individual through the trial. This is what the refinement process looks like for each nature:

Nature	Satan	Process	Product
Submissive	Irritations	Surrounding	Pearl
Stubborn	Sifting	Frictions	Gold
Self-Assured	Boiling	Heat	Gold
Strong-Willed	Pressure	Heat	Diamond

Satan is our capable foe. He has His way of defeating the army of God. The <u>submissive person</u> is like the tank unit of the brigade. Although tanks are surrounded by armor, a small mine or a well-aimed missile can render them useless. This can happen to a submissive person when a combination of many small irritations are interpreted as failure. This failure may make them feel excessively guilty or complacent. Of course, this is when they need to withdraw into God and get His perspective.

Stubborn people are like special forces which are sent in for specific duties. In some cases they are used to scout out strategic points behind enemy lines. Stubborn people's encounters with the enemy can be compared to sniping action, booby traps, mine fields and combat. A constant bombardment of friction not only serves as a means of separation for the stubborn person but it can wear them down. This is when the stubborn person may give way to frustrations, doubts, insecurities and guilt and become vulnerable to the lies and condemnation of Satan. As the cloud of conflict engulfs them, they start to feel hopeless. This hopelessness translates into depression. If they do not allow the Holy Spirit to help them, Satan will keep them out of commission emotionally, until they finally gain the victory in God.

The self-assured individuals serve as the convoy of the spiritual army. Convoys operate on land and sea, and are responsible for getting troops and cargo to designated places in the most secretive and protective ways. They can be handicapped or defeated by covert action such as land mines or torpedos. These attacks can be intensive and drawn out over a long period of time. Self-assured people for instance, can find themselves being boiled in the fire and separated by long-termed illnesses. But, Satan's most effective attacks on these people have to do with their mind and pride. He has been known to use vain imaginations or unrealistic standards to delude them. He can use their pride and anger to torpedo them. It is vital that they allow the truth of Christ to expose any secretive areas of their heart and mind and examine their fruit, attitudes and actions.

The strong-willed people are like the first infantry troops to assault a beach head. They are the most visible people in God's army. Their visibility makes them a big target. Satan throws everything at the strong-willed person because he sees them coming. After all, it is hard to hide the presence of a roaring lion. A strong-willed person must be sensitive to what is going on around him/her, because they tend to have tunnel vision when they are involved in a battle. Satan can deplete their resources by an all out attack, leaving them defenseless and close to destruction. When they are ruled by the Holy Spirit, He serves as their commander and advisor. His instructions enable them to secure the area of their lives which have not come under His control.

The Word tells us that we will have trials and tribulations to build in us the character of Christ. It always amazes me when some Christians act shocked when they encounter tribulations. They treat the war between the flesh and the spirit as a cold war and avoid or resent conflict. There is no room for retreat. This battle is a difficult war which will not be won overnight. No matter how long the battle may be, we must overcome the world, the flesh and Satan in order for Christ to be lifted up in our lives and in the church.

The third cup is kingdom blessing. We must get beyond self and endure the rigors of being a soldier for the King of kings and Lord of lords in order to win the battle and enter the promised land. There, we will find a city made by the hand of God.

The fourth cup has to do with becoming God's people. This involves praise. In Exodus 7:16 God instructs Moses to tell Pharaoh to *"let my people go, so they may worship Him in the desert."* We see that God is calling His people to separate themselves from Egypt. Egypt represents the world. This separation involves a journey of deliverance from the bondage of Egypt to the promised land. This journey included judgments and battles that weeded out those who refused to believe and could not be trusted with the things of God. And why would God go to all this trouble? He wanted a people who would belong to Him and worship Him.

Freedom, deliverance and redemption all add up to praise. God required the children of Israel to offer up sacrifices in the desert. The only sacrifice we can offer up, besides our lives, is praise. To offer our lives is our reasonable service and means of worship. To offer praise at all times becomes a sweet fragrance to our God. Praise implies we know our God and desire to worship Him in Spirit and in Truth. Praise invites the presence of God to be in our midst. God's presence allows us to minister to Him—and to receive his ministry to us.

In Revelation 4, we see the four creatures: lion, ox, man and eagle around the throne of God worshipping Him with the 24 elders. What a picture of what the church needs to be doing in spirit and truth. The truth is, we have a limited understanding of worship. Oh how we need a revelation of our Holy God. He is worthy of all glory and honor, HE IS WORTHY OF TRUE WORSHIP!!

God desires and deserves a special (or peculiar) people who will love Him with all their heart, soul, mind and might. He is looking for righteous individuals who will stand as His priests. He wants temples that are cleansed by the presence of His Living Waters, the Holy Spirit. He wants holy vessels which can be used for His glory. He wants a people who will worship Him no matter what is happening. He wants you and me!

How do we enter into a place of praise and worship? We begin by establishing a relationship with God. Relationship requires communication.

Communion with God

It is a well known fact that relationships break down when there is no communication. Good communication involves meeting on the common ground of trust and respect. It is hard to open yourself up to someone you have nothing in common with, or don't trust or respect.

I listen to Christians emphasize their church, doctrines and sometimes the Holy Spirit, but the Jesus Christ of the Bible is the only acceptable common ground where a Christian will meet God. This common ground enables the Christian to enter into an intimacy with the Father based on the knowledge of Christ. This knowledge will establish the love that binds man together with his/her Creator.

The next vital ingredient in fellowshipping with God is trust. Trust is the same as faith. True faith translates into righteousness because it always responds in obedience.

Respect between God and the believer can be summarized in the fear of the Lord. This fear describes a right attitude before God.

Many Christians feel their prayer life is inadequate. Many times I have seen Christians covet what they perceive to be successful prayer lives of others, and yet people have different prayer lives based on their nature. Part of having an effective prayer life comes from understanding how we approach God and how He ministers to each of us differently. Also by understanding our prayer life, we will know what weaknesses we need to be aware of in our communion with God.

The best way to explain prayer life based on the four natures is to describe it as a wall. We are on the outside of the wall trying to reach God on the other side.

A submissive person does not want to attract a lot of attention, so they will look for a door in the wall. They can be quite tenacious in their search for the door, and once they find it they must climb over their fear to enter in.

God ministers to a submissive person by instructing them in His ways. These people can come out of their prayer closet with great insight into the ways and things of God. This builds their confidence and becomes a source of life which God can use to minister to other people.

Stubborn people are persistent. They see the wall and decide to break right through it. God usually ministers to them through intercessory prayer for others. Since this individual feels they must earn their way, praying for others serves as a means to open the stubborn person up to receive God's blessing.

Intercessory prayer also helps them forget about their feelings. God can show this person much about people's lives and events as a means of ministering to others.

Self-assured people can be persistent when it comes to their prayer life, but they have to climb over their image to allow God to minister to them. God ministers to self-assured people by showing them great and mighty truths about Himself, events and their call. This serves as valuable proof of God's commitment to them. They, in turn, can make the necessary commitment to those around them whether it comes in the form of leadership, intercessory prayer or service to others.

The strong-willed person will jump over the wall to get to God in prayer. God ministers to this individual by bringing a clarity to situations. It is not unusual for this person to see Christ or to hear Him speak decisively to them. The strong-willed person uses this decisiveness to minister the life of Christ to others in any type of ministry.

Have you noticed how each nature ministers according to the way God ministers to them? Therefore, trying to copy another nature closes down the avenue in which all forms of ministry will occur in and through your life.

Each nature must watch for the deceptions of self and Satan. A submissive person can become complacent in their prayer life. They may believe their negative lot comes from God. They may consider this attitude as sincere faith, but it really can come from false humility or a fear of not being accepted by God.

A stubborn person can feel too unworthy to pray because of guilt and condemnation. Sometimes this feeling is due to rebellion or resentment in their life. They feel God does not love them because He is not answering their prayers the way they want Him to, therefore they assume He will reject them if they came into His presence.

A self-assured person can have a list against themselves and God which prevents them from entering into God's presence. They feel that God does not care about them and would not respect their wishes because of their offenses. On the other hand they can take much pride in what they perceived in their prayer time. Some self-assured people have the idea that everything they see is from God because they consult Him about every situation. This can make them appear foolish to those around them because common sense should be sufficient for most daily decisions and activities. Some people feel this is a way for the self-assured person to avoid making decisions and maintaining a facade of super-spirituality in the name of God.

The feeling of infallibility, control and excessive activities can keep the strong-willed person from going to their prayer closet. They have a tendency to believe whatever they think or see in their prayer life is from God. I have seen strong-willed people go contrary to the Word of God and the Spirit, and believe they were spiritually right. I knew one strong-willed pastor who stated that, "Satan never talked to him," but his life declared the opposite fact. It is amazing how these people can delude themselves.

Testing the Spirit

It is important that every Christian test what they perceive in their times of study and their prayer closet. It must line up with the nature and attitude of the Living Word (truth) and have the right spirit.

The main problem people have in their times with God is the assumption that anything they may hear, see or think is from God.

There are, many voices. There is the voice of deceptive pride, which always makes us right and elite in whatever we may perceive while reading the Scriptures, or in times of prayer. There is the voice of Satan who is a clever religious counterfeit. He draws us away from exalting the real Christ into religious gymnastics which make self appear super spiritual or super religious. There are the voices of others who can call us to conform to a religious exterior without any inward transformation. Then, there is the voice of the Spirit who always lead us to the knowledge of Christ. It is the revelation of the real Jesus that works sobriety, (a combination of fear of the Lord and humility) in us.

In the area of sight, our vision can be influenced by personal desires, Satan or the Holy Spirit. I can remember an incident where a young Christian man found his sights focused in on an attractive unbelieving woman. He started out witnessing to her, but eventually began desiring her. As the desire escalated, so did the visions and prophecies concerning a promised future together after she was saved. He saw them married and ministering together. This blessed future was supposedly confirmed by words of knowledge from men of God. In time the relationship exploded in his face bringing him to spiritual ruin for a season. Strong desires with Satan's help can catch us unaware, and supersede God's will and Word.

In another situation a church leader had a dream that two ministers of the Gospel were going to cause divorces among three couples in their church. She went to the leaders of her church, who unwisely told some of the couples involved. This brought suspicion and false accusations against the two ministers who actually were able to reconcile one of the couples. Slander and suspicion always come from the camp of Satan. It is intended to hurt innocent parties and defile the testimony and work of God's servants. This is why all visions and dreams must be tested and verified.

The mind is a subtle place where vain imaginations lurk. I have watched some Christians make their ideas of God's truth secretive or bazaar. The truths of God are simple, only the carnal mind and Satan complicates them.

Now I See God!

Many Christians feel they are standing outside of the abundant life found in Christ. They observe other people enjoying the fruits of this life, and feel left out and unaccepted. God wants to show Himself to them but they must come in and see Him for themselves. They can know His acceptance, love and recognition. In fact, they can know Him.

There are various factors that keep us out. Beliefs, fear, guilt and shame are just a few examples of what keep us from entering into this complete life, and seeing God for ourselves.

God also reveals Himself differently to each nature. God shows Himself to a submissive person in a couple of ways. First, He comes to them in simple ways. I remember a submissive person who had a hard time accepting God's forgiveness. Dark curtains of shame and guilt separated her from seeing Christ. One day she asked Christ to bring those curtains down. Once they came down, she saw Christ reaching out to her in acceptance. In turn she reached out and touched Him. In a joyful cry, she yelled, "I am free! I am free!"

179

Secondly, God can give a submissive person a revelation of Himself from a heavenly perspective. Isaiah and John both witnessed God while He was in His heavenly temple.

The stubborn person sees God in His creation. They sense His power when considering the majesty of His heavens. They see His beauty when they study a flower. They feel His intervention when they ponder life around them.

The stubborn person can and must see Christ in order to feel His love and experience His acceptance. This type of encounter usually occurs when the stubborn individual is forced through desperation to push past their fear, guilt and excuses to see Him. This desperation comes out of some of their darkest times.

Self-assured people usually first see Christ in obscurity. In asking God why, He showed me these people consider Him through their own image. These ideas make Him obscure to them. It is only after they push through their concepts are they able to accept Christ for who He is. Meanwhile as they are pushing through these images, a contrast must be made in order for them to see the difference between the unrealistic standards they have of God and who He really is in spirit and truth.

We see this contrast in the lives of Moses and Job. Moses witnessed many of God's miracles before He saw God on Mount Sinai. At the end of Job's difficult process, God gave Him a clear comparison of His identity. Job made this declaration after God finished with His comparison, *"I heard of God, but now I see Him."*

Strong-willed people will clearly see Christ. Christ reveals Himself to them when they are in great need because of extreme situations, or when their beliefs or conclusions have failed them. A strong-willed person's beliefs will prevent them from seeing God. Once those beliefs are shattered or when the strong-willed person loses control, then God is able to show Himself to them. It is vital that each of us sees God. It is during these times that we sense His love, acceptance and recognition in spite of our pathetic condition. As we realize His commitment to us, we in turn, can accept His life without any reservations. This life is made real to us by the peace we experience because we have peace with our Creator.

21

Jesus is Coming Back!

The greatest message for the church today is that Jesus is coming back for His body,the church. He will be coming for a victorious church, clothed in righteousness and meekness. He is coming for a sanctified body, cleansed by the washing of His Word and purified by the work of His Holy Spirit. He is coming for an overcoming people, set free by the revelation of who He is and healed spiritually by the power of the Holy Spirit. He is coming for a priesthood who is obedient and representative of a high calling. He is coming back for a priceless heirloom comprised of gemstones which reflect His attitude, heart, Lordship and glory to this lost world.

Let us now consider what this heirloom looks like:

Heirloom	Submissive (Pearl)	Stubborn (Gold)	Self-Assured (Gold)	Strong-Willed (Diamond)
Examples in the Word	John Daniel (Eagle)	Peter David (Ox)	Jesus Moses (Man)	Paul Joseph (Lion)
The Rock: Relationship to Christ	Pillar (Standing on Him)	Stone (Aligned to the Corner-stone)	Anointing (Erecting Him in their life)	Judgment (Power-Separation)
Example of Christ (World)	Mind (Submitted)	Heart (Love)	Position (Servitude-Lordship)	Authority (Obedience)
Potential in the Church	Heavenly Perspective	Prophetic Voice	Represent the Real Jesus	To show the work of the Cross

The question is, how dare we fail not to be the gemstones that reflect the light of his life? Matthew 5:13 tells us *"we must make a difference;"* then why do some of us treat much of the Word as an option and not a responsibility? Revelation 21:7 states that *"only those who overcome will eat of the tree of life."* Why do any of us accept a life, which is simply only maintaining until His return?

The church is calling for repentance, but as His body are we willing to pay the price? The head of the body went to the cross, are we willing to follow Him there? Are we willing to suffer and die for the gospel?

There are two fires: the Holy Spirit and persecution. God desires to purify His church with the Spirit but, because of rebellion, He often has to use the fires of persecution. The beauty of revival is that it can begin with one willing heart that allows the fire to purify it.

Many times revival is confused with outward attempts to get God's attention. For example, it is easy to show tears of remorse. But are we willing to allow the Spirit to show us our pride and break us in order to seek God's mercy and forgiveness in spirit and truth? It is easy to fast and pray outwardly, but are we willing to acknowledge we need personal revival because of spiritual famine and independence? We may want revival, but until we put more emphasis on what is going on in our own temples (lives), rather than on religious activities and material things, our labor will be in vain just as it was with Israel during Haggai's time.

Regardless of formulas and outward religious acts and attempts, there is only one door to revival: brokenness of heart and spirit. There is only one revelation that creates such brokenness-- Jesus' nailed pierced hands. There is only one acceptable altar we must go to--the cross. There is only one way we will be stirred up--by the very hand of God.

Jesus is coming back for a church who will be His crowning glory. Therefore, the insignificant grain of sand must be surrounded, the gold separated from the dross and the piece of coal totally changed into the priceless diamond. For there is no other way in which God's people can be set into the crown of the King of kings and Lord of lords.

To order additional copies of "Hidden Manna"
Send $10.00 + $2.00 shipping & handling to:

Gentle Shepherd Ministries
P.O. Box 93 • Nampa, ID 83653-0093
Email: ministry@gentleshepherd.com
www.gentleshepherd.com

Bulk and bookstore discounts available